# Our Lady's Psalter

## A Scriptural Rosary
## and Spiritual Journal

*God bless you!*
*Kathy Romer*

*The Joyful, Sorrowful, and Glorious Mysteries of the Rosary
in the Book of Psalms*

*The Luminous Mysteries of the Rosary
in the Book of Sirach*

Compiled by Kathy Romer

# List of Abbreviations

Acts—Acts of the Apostles
1 Cor—1 Corinthians
CCC—Catechism of the Catholic Church
Eph—Ephesians
Heb—Hebrews
Jam—James
Jn—John
Lk—Luke
Mk—Mark
Mt—Matthew
Phil—Philippians
Rev—Revelation
Rom—Romans
Sir—Sirach
1 Thess—1 Thessalonians
2 Tim—2 Timothy

# Table of Contents

A Book is Born ........................................................................ 8
Introduction to the Rosary ..................................................... 10
Introduction to the Psalms .................................................... 13

*The Joyful Mysteries* (Psalms 1-50) ....................................... 14
   1.  The Annunciation of Gabriel to Mary ....................... 15
   2.  The Visitation of Mary to Elizabeth .......................... 18
   3.  The Birth of Jesus ..................................................... 21
   4.  The Presentation in the Temple ................................ 24
   5.  The Finding of Jesus in the Temple .......................... 27
*The Sorrowful Mysteries* (Psalms 51-100) .............................. 30
   1.  The Agony in the Garden .......................................... 31
   2.  The Scourging at the Pillar ....................................... 34
   3.  The Crowning with Thorns ....................................... 37
   4.  Jesus Carries His Cross ............................................. 40
   5.  The Crucifixion ......................................................... 43
*The Glorious Mysteries* (Psalms 101-150) ............................... 46
   1.  The Resurrection of the Lord ................................... 47
   2.  The Ascension of Jesus into Heaven ......................... 50
   3.  The Descent of the Holy Spirit .................................. 53
   4.  The Assumption of Mary into Heaven ...................... 56
   5.  The Coronation of Mary as Queen of Heaven .......... 59
*The Luminous Mysteries* (Sirach 1-50) ................................... 62
   1.  The Baptism of the Lord ........................................... 63
   2.  The Miracle at Cana ................................................. 66
   3.  The Proclamation of the Kingdom of God ............... 69
   4.  The Transfiguration .................................................. 72
   5.  The Institution of the Holy Eucharist ...................... 75

Appendix A: Prayers of the Rosary ......................................... 78
Appendix B: Scriptural Rosary from the Book of Psalms
             and the Book of Sirach ....................................... 81
   *The Joyful Mysteries* ............................................................ 82
   *The Sorrowful Mysteries* ....................................................... 87
   *The Glorious Mysteries* ......................................................... 92
   *The Luminous Mysteries* ....................................................... 95

*Praying a Rosary is not
an academic exercise,
or even a spiritual exercise.
It is an act of love
for Jesus
and for His mother.*

# A Book is Born

One night, while praying a rosary with my husband Mark, I was reflecting on how the rosary is based on the pattern of the Psalms. I had seen several different Scriptural rosaries (rosaries with a Bible verse for each Hail Mary), but none of them were taken from the Book of Psalms. I wondered if a person could read the Psalms one by one and choose one verse from each Psalm to correspond to each Hail Mary in the Rosary?

After we finished our rosary that night, I decided to look at the Psalms, and was captivated by how simple it was to find verses that were appropriate for the Annunciation (the first Joyful mystery) in the first ten Psalms, and then verses that were appropriate for the Visitation in the next ten, and so on. It was so shockingly simple, in fact, that I had chosen verses from all 150 Psalms - in order - in about two days, in my spare time. I do not attribute this ease to any skill on my part; it simply seemed plain to one looking for it.

Sometimes while reading through a Psalm, I would think to myself, "Virtually any passage from this Psalm would fit what I need." But occasionally I would read a Psalm and worry, "Nothing fits this mystery. What's happening?" Suddenly, however, the tone of the Psalm would change completely and the appropriate verse would present itself.

Of course, it is no coincidence that Jesus' life should be detailed in this way, since Jesus told his disciples (in the Gospel according to Luke), "These are my words that I spoke to you while I was still with you, that everything written about me in the law of Moses and in the prophets and *psalms* must be fulfilled" (Lk 24:44,45, emphasis added). It took another three to four days to choose New Testament references for the Psalm verses, attempting to show why I had preferred a particular Psalm verse for a particular Mystery.

Except for typing the verses on my computer in a Scriptural Rosary form, I set the project aside for many years. I had contacted some publishers about it, but interest was low for "just another Scriptural Rosary". As I said, that was several years ago; but recently God has sent several people into my life who prompted me to finish to what I had begun.

One of those people was my friend, Amy. She and I attended a faith-sharing group, and during the course of our meetings, I told Amy and the others about this phenomenon within the Psalms, and gave them copies of what I had done so far. Amy was very enthusiastic, but recommended that before I give a copy to anyone else that I should expand it into a more thorough book form: taking each mystery one at a time and breaking it down, showing the full text of the Psalm verse that I had chosen as well as the full verse of the explanatory New Testament reference, and adding a brief commentary about each pair of verses. (I had originally thought that a more extensive book would be the best approach, but I was hoping to get away with less work!) A brief reflection after each Mystery seemed more appropriate after all, since breaking it down into each pair of verses became too distracting from the praying of the Rosary, which is the main intent of the meditation.

I also had a talk with a local priest, on what I thought at the time was an unrelated issue. I was "treading water" in my prayer life; I was not drawing closer to Christ. He suggested that I use Scripture as a basis for meditative prayer; reading one or two verses from Scripture, and asking questions about them: for example, what is Jesus telling me in this verse, how might it apply to my life, what should I do about it, etc.

After some thought, I realized that this was essentially what I would be doing if I were to expand these Psalm and New Testament verses into book form. In writing my thoughts on these verses, I would not only be finishing this project, but I would also be drawing closer to Christ.

The irony was that I was so entrenched in the academic side of the project that I couldn't think of any spiritual insights! The Spiritual Advisor for our diocesan Cursillo Movement gave me inspiration by suggesting that instead of mere insights, I write a prayer after each mystery.

And finally, I owe a debt of gratitude to my friends, Cecelia and Mark, who sought the Holy Spirit's counsel in adding some of the reflections within this book.

## Introduction to the Rosary

For almost two thousand years, Catholic priests and religious have read and prayed the Book of Psalms. This practice of praying the Psalms is itself preserved from our Jewish heritage. Within the Catholic Church, this exercise is called the Divine Office, or the Psalter. According to one version of how the Rosary evolved to its current state, during the Middle Ages, the Catholic laity asked for help to increase their devotion to God. They, too, wanted to pray the Psalms in the ways that the priests and religious did.

Unfortunately, since the printing press had not yet been invented, most people of that time did not have access to books. Many times even a monastery only had one copy of the Bible, which was read aloud at common prayer times. Although efforts were being made by the Church to teach her faithful both spiritually and academically, it was not practical at the time to make hand-printed copies of the Psalms for everyone. Nor was it expected that every layperson (or even every scholar) could memorize all 150 Psalms.

In order to help the laity realize their ambition of deeper spirituality, the Dominican order of priests chose 15 events from the lives of Jesus and Mary – ranging from the angel's announcement to Mary about Jesus' conception to the coronation of Mary in heaven by her Son. The priests encouraged meditation on each of these events (often called "mysteries" because belief in them is a gift of faith).

As an aid to meditation and to keep the pattern of 150 prayers, the priests promoted praying ten "Salutations to the Blessed Mother" during the meditation of each event, equaling 150 Salutations to represent the 150 Psalms. The title for the prayer "Salutations to the Blessed Mother" was later shortened to the more affectionate "Hail Mary" (the first two words of the prayer).

This set of prayers and meditations came to be known as the "rosary," comparing these prayers to a bouquet of roses offered to God. It was also called Our Lady's Psalter, to show the connection to the Psalms that the priests prayed in the Divine Office.

Thanks to the modern printing press, we now have copies of the Psalms (indeed, of the entire Bible) for almost any person who wishes to pray the Divine Office as priests do. However, the rosary itself is a wonderful practice, drawing the mind of the devoted person into contemplation on the lives of Jesus and His mother. The rosary in this book combines the two practices by selecting one verse from each Psalm to correspond to the mysteries of the rosary.

Although a rosary has many prayers repeated over and over, it is **not** meant to induce a trance-like state. It is a prayer to God, which is dialogue with God. A prayer is a conversation, and it is intended to bring the heart, mind, and soul closer to God. Just as Jesus was able to repeat the prayer "Father, not my will but thine be done" (during His agony in the garden of Gethsemane the night before His death) without any loss of fervor or devotion, so the person who prays the rosary is expected to be able to mean what he or she prays each time a prayer is repeated.

This fervor is particularly aided by the Scripture verses that accompany each Hail Mary, but should also be achieved without the verses. Concentration is necessary as the prayer is prayed; with each recitation of the prayer, one should reflect anew on the words. It is sometimes helpful to emphasize different words during one Hail Mary than on another as an aid to this concentration.

A rosary begins with the Apostles' Creed. This is a profession of faith named for its link to the beliefs of the early Christians. The words of this creed, as well as all the prayers of the rosary, can be found in Appendix A at the end of this book.

There are other introductory prayers, which include the Lord's Prayer (usually called the "Our Father" because those are the first two words in the prayer) taken from Matthew 6:9-13. It is also customary to say three Hail Marys and one Gloria (usually referred to as the "Glory be to the Father" or simply the "Glory Be," the first words of that prayer) before beginning meditations on the mysteries.

The rosary is further segmented into three sets of five mysteries, concentrating on different aspects of the lives of Jesus and Mary. These sets are commonly called the Joyful, Sorrowful, and Glorious mysteries. The Joyful mysteries encourage meditation on Jesus' early life; while the Sorrowful mysteries detail the Passion of Christ; and the Glorious mysteries deal with the Resurrection of Jesus and events after that. Each mystery begins with one Our Father, followed by ten Hail Marys, then one Glory Be, and finally the Fatima Prayer (see below) at the end of the mystery.

The "Fatima Prayer" was added at the end of each mystery after the apparition of the Blessed Virgin Mary at Fatima, Portugal, in 1917. There, Mary asked three young children to pray an extra prayer at the end of each mystery of the rosary. Once the apparition was declared genuine by the Church, sanction was given to all the faithful to add this prayer as a pious exercise to the rosary. This prayer begins with the words "O my Jesus, forgive us..." and that is how I have designated in the rosary to begin that prayer.

In October of 2002, Pope John Paul II instituted a new set of mysteries to the rosary, called the Luminous mysteries. These mysteries encompass Jesus' life of public ministry, beginning with His baptism by John and continuing to the Institution of the Holy Eucharist the night before His death.

I had already used the entire Book of Psalms for the Joyful, Sorrowful, and Glorious mysteries; so I looked for another book of the Bible with exactly fifty chapters to fit the Luminous mysteries. The Book of Sirach turned out to be the perfect choice.

The main body of the book shows verses from both the Old and New Testaments together for each mystery of the rosary. For those who may want to read only the Psalm verses for each mystery, Appendix B is written with only the accompanying Psalm verse (except for the Luminous mysteries, which have verses taken from the Book of Sirach). Following the verse attribution, the reader can find the New Testament reference for the Psalm quotation in parentheses.

Since the verses from the Books of Sirach and Psalms do not necessarily occur in the same order as the New Testament sequence within each mystery, the reader will find that sometimes the New Testament references skip back and forth.

Another help for concentrating during the mysteries of the rosary is to pray for certain virtues (sometimes referred to as "fruits" of a mystery), or for prayer intentions that are appropriate for that particular mystery. I have placed the traditional fruit for each mystery before the Lord's Prayer.

## Introduction to the Psalms

The Psalms were written, like many books of the Old Testament, over a period of many years by many different authors. However, approximately half of the Psalms are attributed to King David.

Some of the Psalms were written to be sung within the context of a liturgy, while others are personal in nature. Some Psalms are lamentations; some are songs of praise; some of thanksgiving.

# The Joyful Mysteries

The Joyful mysteries cover the time from the angel's announcement of Jesus' birth to Mary through Jesus' early life. The first mystery is called the Annunciation, a fancy word for the announcement from the angel Gabriel to the Virgin Mary about the conception of Jesus. The angel also tells Mary that her kinswoman, Elizabeth, has conceived a child in her old age.

The second mystery, the Visitation, is Mary's visit to Elizabeth to help her elderly cousin during the last three months of her pregnancy, as well as to share in her joy.

The Birth of Jesus is the third mystery, and it deals with several events: Jesus' birth, the angels' song of praise that roused the shepherds to find Jesus, and the magi's search for the child.

The fourth mystery, known as the Presentation in the Temple, speaks of a holy man, Simeon, and a prophetess, Anna. Under the inspiration of the Holy Spirit, both come to the Temple on the day that Mary and Joseph bring Jesus there as a baby.

The Finding in the Temple is the name of the fifth mystery. It details how Jesus – at twelve years old – stayed behind in Jerusalem after Passover without his parents' knowledge, and how he was found by them after three days.

## *Apostle's Creed*
## *Our Father; 3 Hail Marys; Glory Be*

## The First Joyful Mystery:
## **The Annunciation of Gabriel to Mary**

The angel Gabriel appears to Mary. He announces that she will conceive and bear a son—and yet still remain a virgin. The child shall be called Jesus. Gabriel also tells Mary that her relative Elizabeth is with child. The angel's greeting to Mary (found in Luke 1:28) makes up the first line of the "Hail Mary" prayer.

*Fruit of the mystery: humility.*

### *Our Father*

*Psalm 1:2*    [Happy the man who] the law of the LORD is their joy;
        God's law they study day and night.

*Luke 1:26,27*    In the sixth month, the angel Gabriel was sent from God to a town of Galilee called Nazareth, to a virgin betrothed to a man named Joseph, of the house of David, and the virgin's name was Mary.

### *Hail Mary*

*Psalm 2:7*    I will proclaim the decree of the LORD,
        who said to me, "You are my son;
        today I am your father."

*Luke 1:30,31*    Then the angel said to [Mary], "Do not be afraid, Mary, for you have found favor with God. Behold, you will conceive in your womb and bear a son, and you shall name him Jesus."

### *Hail Mary*

*Psalm 3:9*    Safety comes from the LORD!
        Your blessing for your people!

*Luke 1:32*    [The angel said,] "He will be great and will be called Son of the Most High, and the Lord God will give him the throne of David his father."

### *Hail Mary*

*Psalm 4:4*    Know that the LORD works wonders for the faithful;
        the LORD hears when I call out.

*Luke 1:34*    But Mary said to the angel, "How can this be, since I have no relations with a man?"

### *Hail Mary*

**Psalm 5:8**  But I can enter your house
because of your great love.
I can worship in your holy temple
because of my reverence for you, LORD.

**Luke 1:35**  And the angel said to her in reply, "The holy Spirit will come
upon you, and the power of the Most High will overshadow
you. Therefore the child to be born will be called holy, the
Son of God."

*Hail Mary*

**Psalm 6:10**  The LORD has heard my prayer;
the LORD takes up my plea.

**Luke 1:36**  [The angel said,] "And behold, Elizabeth, your relative, has
also conceived a son in her old age, and this is the sixth
month for her who was called barren."

*Hail Mary*

**Psalm 7:9**  O LORD, judge of the nations.
Grant me justice, LORD, for I am blameless,
free of any guilt.

**Luke 1:26-28**  In the sixth month, the angel Gabriel was sent from God to ...
Mary. And coming to her, he said, "Hail, favored one! The
Lord is with you."

*Hail Mary*

**Psalm 8:2**  O LORD, our Lord,
how awesome is your name through all the earth!
You have set your majesty above the heavens!

**Luke 1:32**  [The angel said,] "He will be great and will be called Son of
the Most High, and the Lord God will give him the throne of
David his father."

*Hail Mary*

**Psalm 9:11**  Those who honor your name trust in you;
a stronghold in times of trouble.

**Luke 1:37**  [The angel said,] "For nothing will be impossible for God."

*Hail Mary*

**Psalm 10:16**  The LORD is king forever;
the nations have vanished from God's land.

**Luke 1:38**  Mary said, "Behold, I am the handmaid of the Lord. May it be
done to me according to your word." Then the angel
departed from her.

*Hail Mary; Glory Be...*
*O My Jesus, forgive us...*

## Reflections:

In the Gospel according to Luke, we are told that the words "Hail, favored one!" are addressed to Mary by the angel Gabriel. What we are **not** told is—anything else!! For example, where is Mary when the angel speaks to her? What is she doing? Is she alone? Can she see Gabriel, or does she simply hear his voice? All the juicy tidbits that would make for an exciting—and thus distracting— narrative are completely stripped away: only the essence is kept: a voice in greeting, "Hail, favored one."

The first line of the "Hail, Mary" prayer is taken from this line of Scripture. The Latin translation of the original text was "full of grace," and so the first line of the prayer is "Hail, Mary, full of grace." However, in addition to being "full of grace," Mary in her surprised state was full of humility, as well. She knew that any grace was hers by God's favor.

Which verse touched your heart? Why?

What has God done to accomplish the impossible in your life?

## The Second Joyful Mystery:
### The Visitation of Mary to Elizabeth

Mary goes to visit her cousin, Elizabeth, and together they marvel at the Lord's favor toward them. Elizabeth's greeting to Mary (found in Luke 1:42) makes up the second line of the "Hail Mary" prayer.

*Fruit of the mystery: charity.*

*Our Father*

*Psalm 11:4*  The LORD is in his holy temple;
the LORD's throne is in heaven.
God's eyes keep careful watch,
they test all peoples.

*Luke 1:41,42*  When Elizabeth heard Mary's greeting, the infant leaped in her womb, and Elizabeth, filled with the holy Spirit, cried out in a loud voice and said, "Most blessed are you among women, and blessed is the fruit of your womb."

*Hail Mary*

*Psalm 12:7*  The promises of the LORD are sure,
silver refined in a crucible,
silver purified seven times.

*Luke 1:45*  [Elizabeth said,] "Blessed are you who believed that what was spoken to you by the Lord would be fulfilled."

*Hail Mary*

*Psalm 13:6*  I trust in your faithfulness.
Grant my heart joy in your help,
That I may sing of the LORD,
"How good our God has been to me!"

*Luke 1:46,47*  And Mary said:
"My soul proclaims the greatness of the Lord;
my spirit rejoices in God my savior."

*Hail Mary*

*Psalm 14:7*  Oh, that from Zion might come
the deliverance of Israel,
That Jacob may rejoice and Israel be glad
when the LORD restores his people!

*Luke 1:49*  [Mary said,] "The Mighty One has done great things for me,
and holy is his name."

*Hail Mary*

*Psalm 15:2*  Whoever walks without blame,
doing what is right,
speaking truth from the heart.

*Luke 1:50*  [Mary said,] "His mercy is from age to age
to those who fear him."

*Hail Mary*

| | |
|---|---|
| *Psalm 16:9* | Therefore my heart is glad, my soul rejoices; <br> my body also dwells secure. |
| *Luke 1:48* | [Mary said,] "For he has looked upon his handmaid's lowliness; <br> behold, from now on will all ages call me blessed." |

*Hail Mary*

| | |
|---|---|
| *Psalm 17:8* | Keep me as the apple of your eye; <br> hide me in the shadow of your wings. |
| *Luke 1:48* | [Mary said,] "For he has looked upon his handmaid's lowliness; <br> behold, from now on will all ages call me blessed." |

*Hail Mary*

| | |
|---|---|
| *Psalm 18:50* | Thus I will proclaim you, LORD, among the nations; <br> I will sing the praises of your name. |
| *Luke 1:49* | [Mary said,] "The Mighty One has done great things for me, <br> and holy is his name." |

*Hail Mary*

| | |
|---|---|
| *Psalm 19:15* | Let the words of my mouth meet with your favor, <br> keep the thoughts of my heart before you, <br> LORD, my rock and my redeemer. |
| *Luke 1:41,42* | When Elizabeth heard Mary's greeting, the infant leaped in her womb, and Elizabeth, filled with the holy Spirit, cried out in a loud voice and said, "Most blessed are you among women, and blessed is the fruit of your womb." |

*Hail Mary*

| | |
|---|---|
| *Psalm 20:7* | Now I know victory is given <br> to the anointed of the LORD. <br> God will answer him from the holy heavens <br> with a strong arm that brings victory. |
| *Luke 1:54,55* | [Mary said,] "He has helped Israel his servant, <br> remembering his mercy, <br> according to his promise to our fathers, <br> to Abraham and to his descendants forever." |

*Hail Mary; Glory Be...*
*O My Jesus, forgive us...*

## Reflections:

The mutual joy shared by Mary and Elizabeth has two components. The first is the simple human happiness of expectation for the new lives of John the Baptist and Jesus. But above the human happiness, these women shared the spiritual joy of God's special blessing on their pregnancies. Neither woman was "supposed" to get pregnant, but God showed His favor on them.

Which verse touched your heart? Why?

Is there anyone in your life that God is calling you to visit?

## The Third Joyful Mystery:
### The Birth of Jesus

God comes to earth in the form of the infant Jesus. The angels sing his praise and rouse the shepherds to find Him, and magi come from the east and seek to worship him. The verse of Luke 2:11 tells us that Mary's baby Jesus is both "Messiah and Lord". That is why the third line of the "Hail Mary" prayer calls Mary the "Mother of God".

*Fruit of the mystery: love of poverty.*

*Our Father*

**Psalm 21:7**
You make him the pattern of blessings forever;
   you gladden him with the joy of your presence.

**Luke 2:6,7**
While they were there, the time came for her to have her child, and she gave birth to her firstborn son. She wrapped him in swaddling clothes and laid him in a manger, because there was no room for them in the inn.

*Hail Mary*

**Psalm 22:24**
You who fear the LORD, give praise!
   All descendants of Jacob, give honor;
   show reverence, all descendants of Israel!

**Luke 2:8**
Now there were shepherds in that region living in the fields and keeping the night watch over their flock.

*Hail Mary*

**Psalm 23:6**
Only goodness and love will pursue me
   all the days of my life;
I will dwell in the house of the LORD
   for years to come.

**Luke 2:11**
[The angel said,] "For today in the city of David a savior has been born for you who is Messiah and Lord."

*Hail Mary*

**Psalm 24:10**
Who is this king of glory?
   The LORD of hosts is the king of glory.

**Luke 2:13,14**
And suddenly there was a multitude of the heavenly host with the angel, praising God and saying:
"Glory to God in the highest
   and on earth peace to those on whom his favor rests."

*Hail Mary*

**Psalm 25:5**
Guide me in your truth and teach me,
   for you are God my savior.
For you I wait all the long day,
   because of your goodness, LORD.

*Matthew 2:1,2*   When Jesus was born in Bethlehem of Judea, in the days of King Herod, behold, magi from the east arrived in Jerusalem, saying, "Where is the newborn king of the Jews? We saw his star at its rising and have come to do him homage."
*Hail Mary*

*Psalm 26:3*   Your love is before my eyes;
I walk guided by your faithfulness.

*Matthew 2:10,11* They were overjoyed at seeing the star, and on entering the house they saw the child with Mary his mother. They prostrated themselves and did him homage. Then they opened their treasures and offered him gifts of gold, frankincense, and myrrh.
*Hail Mary*

*Psalm 27:8*   "Come," says my heart, "seek God's face";
your face, LORD, do I seek!

*Luke 2:15*   When the angels went away from them to heaven, the shepherds said to one another, "Let us go, then, to Bethlehem to see this thing that has taken place, which the Lord has made known to us."
*Hail Mary*

*Psalm 28:7*   The LORD is my strength and my shield,
in whom my heart trusted and found help.
So my heart rejoices;
with my song I praise my God.

*Luke 2:20*   Then the shepherds returned, glorifying and praising God for all they had heard and seen, just as it had been told to them.
*Hail Mary*

*Psalm 29:2*   Give to the LORD the glory due God's name.
Bow down before the LORD's holy splendor!

*Luke 2:13*   And suddenly there was a multitude of the heavenly host with the angel, praising God.
*Hail Mary*

*Psalm 30:13*   With my whole being I sing
endless praise to you.
O LORD, my God,
forever will I give you thanks.

*Luke 2:14*   [The host of angels sang,] "Glory to God in the highest and on earth peace to those on whom his favor rests."
*Hail Mary; Glory Be...*
*O My Jesus, forgive us...*

## Reflections:

The angel tells Mary, "the Lord is with you." Sometimes when I pray the Hail Mary, I say that line with a little wistful sigh, "Oh, sure, Mary, the Lord is with *you*, of course! You were so holy and pure." When I think like that, I am missing the point of the Scripture passage. I need to believe—because it is true—that the Lord wants to be with me, as well; and actually is with me, when I am in a state of grace.

Which verse touched your heart? Why?

Where has Jesus appeared in your life in a startling way?

## The Fourth Joyful Mystery:
### The Presentation in the Temple

Joseph and Mary present Jesus in the Temple of Jerusalem. A holy man named Simeon, who was waiting for the Messiah and had been promised sight of Him before his death, approaches the holy Family to praise God for Jesus' coming. A prophetess, Anna, also rejoices to see Jesus.
*Fruit of the mystery: obedience.*

*Our Father*

**Psalm 31:6**      Into your hands I commend my spirit;
     you will redeem me, LORD, faithful God.

**Luke 2:29**      [Simeon said,] "Now, Master, you may let your servant go
     in peace, according to your word."

*Hail Mary*

**Psalm 32:11**      Be glad in the LORD and rejoice, you just;
     exult, all you upright of heart.

**Luke 2:25**      Now there was a man in Jerusalem whose name was Simeon. This man was righteous and devout, awaiting the consolation of Israel, and the holy Spirit was upon him.

*Hail Mary*

**Psalm 33:15**      The one who fashioned the hearts of them all
     knows all their works.

**Luke 2:26**      It had been revealed to him by the holy Spirit that he should not see death before he had seen the Messiah of the Lord.

*Hail Mary*

**Psalm 34:6**      Look to God that you may be radiant with joy
     and your faces may not blush for shame.

**Luke 2:30**      [Simeon said,] "For my eyes have seen your salvation."

*Hail Mary*

**Psalm 35:27**      But let those who favor my just cause
     shout for joy and be glad.
     May they ever say, "Exalted be the LORD
     who delights in the peace of his loyal servant."

**Luke 2:28**      [Simeon] took him into his arms and blessed God.

*Hail Mary*

**Psalm 36:11**      Continue your kindness toward your friends,
     your just defense of the honest heart.

**Luke 2:38**      And coming forward at that very time, [Anna] gave thanks to God and spoke about the child to all who were awaiting the redemption of Jerusalem.

*Hail Mary*

| | |
|---|---|
| *Psalm 37:39* | The salvation of the just is from the LORD, |
| | their refuge in time of distress. |
| *Luke 2:32* | [Simeon said,] "A light for revelation to the Gentiles, |
| | and glory for your people Israel." |

*Hail Mary*

| | |
|---|---|
| *Psalm 38:16* | LORD, I wait for you; |
| | O Lord, my God, answer me. |
| *Luke 2:25* | Now there was a man in Jerusalem whose name was Simeon. This man was righteous and devout, awaiting the consolation of Israel, and the holy Spirit was upon him. |

*Hail Mary*

| | |
|---|---|
| *Psalm 39:8* | And now, Lord, what future do I have? |
| | You are my only hope. |
| *Luke 2:26* | It had been revealed to him by the holy Spirit that he should not see death before he had seen the Messiah of the Lord. |

*Hail Mary*

| | |
|---|---|
| *Psalm 40:2* | I waited, waited for the LORD; |
| | who bent down and heard my cry. |
| *Luke 2:29* | [Simeon said,] "Now, Master, you may let your servant go in peace, according to your word." |

*Hail Mary; Glory Be...*
*O My Jesus, forgive us...*

## Reflections:

When Mary went to visit Elizabeth, Elizabeth told her, "blessed is the fruit of your womb." In the Hail Mary prayer, we add the name, "Jesus," to this statement (because we have a little "insider information"—we know Jesus' name; at the time, Elizabeth did not). The prophets Simeon and Anna repeat in different words the great gift it is that Mary has given birth to Jesus. But Simeon also warns Mary that her life will not be without its share of sorrows as well.

Which verse touched your heart? Why?

Share a time when you just had to tell someone about your joy in the Lord's blessings to you.

## The Fifth Joyful Mystery:
### The Finding of Jesus in the Temple

Joseph goes to Jerusalem with Mary and Jesus for the celebration of Passover. Jesus, who is twelve years old at the time, remains in Jerusalem after His family's caravan departs, unbeknownst to Joseph and Mary. Jesus' parents return and find him after three days of searching. He is in the Temple talking with the teachers, and all are amazed at His wisdom.

*Fruit of the mystery: piety.*

### Our Father

**Psalm 41:13**  For my integrity you have supported me
and let me stand in your presence forever.

**Luke 2:40**  The child [Jesus] grew and became strong, filled with wisdom; and the favor of God was upon him.

### Hail Mary

**Psalm 42:5**  Those times I recall
as I pour out my soul,
When I went in procession with the crowd,
I went with them to the house of God,
Amid loud cries of thanksgiving,
with the multitude keeping festival.

**Luke 2:41,42**  Each year [Jesus'] parents went to Jerusalem for the feast of Passover, and when he was twelve years old, they went up according to festival custom.

### Hail Mary

**Psalm 43:4**  That I may come to the altar of God,
to God, my joy, my delight.
Then I will praise you with the harp,
O God, my God.

**Luke 2:43**  After they had completed [the days of Passover], as they were returning, the boy Jesus remained behind in Jerusalem, but his parents did not know it.

### Hail Mary

**Psalm 44:2**  O God, we have heard with our own ears;
our ancestors have told us
The deeds you did in their days,
with your own hand in days of old.

**Luke 2:46**  After three days they found him in the temple, sitting in the midst of the teachers, listening to them and asking them questions.

### Hail Mary

| | |
|---|---|
| *Psalm 45:18* | I will make your name renowned through all generations; the nations shall praise you forever. |
| *Luke 2:47* | And all who heard [Jesus] were astounded at his understanding and his answers. |

*Hail Mary*

| | |
|---|---|
| *Psalm 46:9* | Come and see the works of the LORD, who has done fearsome deeds on earth. |
| *Luke 2:49* | And [Jesus] said to them, "Why were you looking for me? Did you not know that I must be in my Father's house?" |

*Hail Mary*

| | |
|---|---|
| *Psalm 47:5* | Who chose a land for our heritage, the glory of Jacob, the beloved. |
| *Luke 2:50* | But [Joseph and Mary] did not understand what he said to them. |

*Hail Mary*

| | |
|---|---|
| *Psalm 48:10* | O God, within your temple we ponder your steadfast love. |
| *Luke 2:47* | And all who heard [Jesus] were astounded at his understanding and his answers. |

*Hail Mary*

| | |
|---|---|
| *Psalm 49:4* | My mouth shall speak wisdom, my heart shall offer insight. |
| *Luke 2:52* | And Jesus advanced [in] wisdom and age and favor before God and man. |

*Hail Mary*

| | |
|---|---|
| *Psalm 50:7* | "Listen, my people, I will speak; Israel, I will testify against you; God, your God, am I." |
| *Luke 2:46,47* | After three days they found [Jesus] in the temple, sitting in the midst of the teachers, listening to them and asking them questions, and all who heard him were astounded at his understanding and his answers. |

*Hail Mary; Glory Be...*
*O My Jesus, forgive us...*
*Hail, Holy Queen*

## Reflections:

A good friend of mine, who has two teenage boys of her own, made a wry statement after reading this story from Scripture. She said, "Jesus was a teenager, all right! Here are Mary and Joseph, panicked and frantically searching Jerusalem for their Son. And when they find Him, what does Jesus do? He asks what all the fuss is about!" But, naturally, it is a lesson, as well. When we trust that God is in charge, we don't have a care in the world.

Which verse touched your heart? Why?

Name a special time when you found Jesus "in the temple".

# The Sorrowful Mysteries

The Sorrowful mysteries describe the Passion and Death of Christ. The mysteries include:

1. The Agony in the Garden,
2. The Scourging at the Pillar,
3. The Crowning with Thorns,
4. The Carrying of the Cross, and
5. The Crucifixion.

The Agony in the Garden not only includes Jesus' torment in prayer, but his betrayal by Judas, and the trial before the Sanhedrin.

The Scourging at the Pillar details Jesus' trial before Pilate and the beating he endured before the crucifixion.

The Crowning with Thorns has always seemed to me to be a particularly sorrowful mystery. Jesus is being mocked in his role as King, which He is: yet He submits to this abuse in noble silence.

The mystery of the Carrying of the Cross details the nailing of his hands and feet to the cross.

Finally, the Crucifixion describes events surrounding his crucifixion: the forgiveness of the repentant thief, entrusting His Mother to his beloved disciple, and the acclamation of the guard at Jesus' death.

As I read the Psalms, to find verses for the Sorrowful mysteries, I saw that the passages became more and more sad. I had expected this: the events leading up to the Crucifixion were dark and sinful stains upon our world.

And then it was time to find the final ten verses—the ones for the mystery of the Crucifixion. I imagined that these verses would be the saddest of all verses, describing as they would the death of Our Lord.

Was I surprised! It became quite clear that the ten Psalms coinciding with the Crucifixion are jubilant! They speak of glory and salvation and God's blessings for us! It was a wonderful affirmation that Jesus' death on the Cross was the means of our salvation.

# The First Sorrowful Mystery:
## The Agony in the Garden

Jesus prays for strength to endure his trial and death; Judas betrays Him, and the Pharisees unjustly condemn Jesus to death.
*Fruit of the mystery: true contrition.*

*Our Father*

*Psalm 51:13*    Do not drive me from your presence,
                    nor take from me your holy spirit.

*Luke 22:40*    When [Jesus] arrived at the place he said to [the apostles], "Pray that you may not undergo the test."

*Hail Mary*

*Psalm 52:10*    But I, like an olive tree in the house of God,
                    trust in God's faithful love forever.

*Matthew 26:39*    [Jesus] advanced a little and fell prostrate in prayer, saying, "My Father, if it is possible, let this cup pass from me; yet, not as I will, but as you will."

*Hail Mary*

*Psalm 53:7*    Oh, that from Zion might come
                    the deliverance of Israel,
    That Jacob may rejoice and Israel be glad
                    when God restores the people!

*John 18:4,5*    Jesus, knowing everything that was going to happen to him, went out and said to [the mob], "Whom are you looking for?" They answered him, "Jesus the Nazorean." He said to them, "I AM."

*Hail Mary*

*Psalm 54:6*    God is present as my helper;
                    the Lord sustains my life.

*Luke 22:43*    And to strengthen [Jesus] an angel from heaven appeared to him.

*Hail Mary*

*Psalm 55:13,15*    If an enemy had reviled me,
                    that I could bear;
    If my foe had viewed me with contempt,
                    from that I could hide.
    [But not from] you, whose company I enjoyed;
                    at whose side I walked
                    in procession in the house of God!

*Luke 22:47,48*   While [Jesus] was still speaking, a crowd approached and in front was one of the Twelve, a man named Judas. He went up to Jesus to kiss him. Jesus said to him, "Judas, are you betraying the Son of Man with a kiss?"
*Hail Mary*

*Psalm 56:7*   They hide together in ambush;
    they watch my every step;
  they lie in wait for my life.

*Luke 22:1-2*   Now the feast of Unleavened Bread, called the Passover, was drawing near, and the chief priests and the scribes were seeking a way to put [Jesus] to death, for they were afraid of the people.
*Hail Mary*

*Psalm 57:7*   They have set a trap for my feet;
    my soul is bowed down;
  They have dug a pit before me.
    May they fall into it themselves!

*Luke 22:3-4*   Then Satan entered into Judas, the one surnamed Iscariot, who was counted among the Twelve, and he went to the chief priests and temple guards to discuss a plan for handing [Jesus] over to them.
*Hail Mary*

*Psalm 58:2,3*   Do you indeed pronounce justice, O gods;
    do you judge mortals fairly?
  No, you freely engage in crime;
    your hands dispense violence to the earth.

*Mark 14:63,64*   At that the high priest tore his garments and said, "What further need have we of witnesses? You have heard the blasphemy. What do you think?" They all condemned [Jesus] as deserving to die.
*Hail Mary*

*Psalm 59:4*   They have set an ambush for my life;
    the powerful conspire against me.
  For no offense or misdeed of mine, LORD.

*Luke 23:47*   The centurion who witnessed what had happened glorified God and said, "This man was innocent beyond doubt."
*Hail Mary*

*Psalm 60:13*   Give us aid against the foe;
    worthless is human help.

*Mark 14:50*   And [his followers] all left [Jesus] and fled.
*Hail Mary; Glory Be...*
*O My Jesus, forgive us...*

## Reflections:

Dearest Lord Jesus, Your strength and charity during this scene amaze me. Even knowing that you are God, Your humanity must have been supremely frightened, lonely, and sad. Especially knowing, as You did, what was to come: the pain, the mockery, the wickedness that You would endure. I bless You and praise You and ask for some share in Your bravery, that I may also love without limits. Amen.

Which verse touched your heart? Why?

Has someone you loved broken your heart? Share your sadness with Jesus; He knows how you feel.

## The Second Sorrowful Mystery:
### The Scourging at the Pillar

Pilate interrogates Jesus and finds him innocent, but the people call for his death and Pilate accedes to their demands. He has Jesus scourged before the crucifixion so that He will not take too long to die on the cross.
*Fruit of the mystery: purity.*

*Our Father*

**Psalm 61:2**      Hear my cry, O God,
                    listen to my prayer!
**Matthew 26:64**   Jesus said..., "You have said so. But I tell you:
                    From now on you will see 'the Son of Man
                    seated at the right hand of the Power'
                    and 'coming on the clouds of heaven.'"
*Hail Mary*

**Psalm 62:4**      How long will you set upon people,
                    all of you beating them down,
                    As though they were a sagging fence
                    or a battered wall?
**Mark 15:15**      So Pilate, ... after he had Jesus scourged, handed him over to be crucified.
*Hail Mary*

**Psalm 63:9**      My soul clings fast to you;
                    your right hand upholds me.
**John 18:11**      Jesus said to Peter, "...Shall I not drink the cup that the Father gave me?"
*Hail Mary*

**Psalm 64:7**      They devise wicked schemes,
                    conceal the schemes they devise;
                    the designs of their hearts are hidden.
**Matthew 27:17,18**   So when [the crowd] had assembled, Pilate said to them, "Which one do you want me to release to you, [Jesus] Barabbas, or Jesus called Messiah?" For he knew that it was out of envy that they had handed him over.
*Hail Mary*

**Psalm 65:4b**     We are overcome by our sins;
                    only you can pardon them.
**Matthew 27:25**   And the whole people said in reply, "His blood be upon us and upon our children."
*Hail Mary*

| | |
|---|---|
| *Psalm 66:11* | You led us into a snare;<br>    you bound us at the waist as captives. |
| *Matthew 27:20* | The chief priests and the elders persuaded the crowds to ask for Barabbas but to destroy Jesus. |

*Hail Mary*

| | |
|---|---|
| *Psalm 67:3* | So shall your rule be known upon the earth,<br>    your saving power among all the nations. |
| *John 18:20,21* | Jesus answered [the high priest], "I have spoken publicly to the world. I have always taught in a synagogue or in the temple area where all the Jews gather, and in secret I have said nothing. Why ask me? Ask those who heard me what I said to them. They know what I said." |

*Hail Mary*

| | |
|---|---|
| *Psalm 68:20* | Blessed be the Lord day by day,<br>    God, our salvation, who carries us. |
| *Matthew 8:16,17* | When it was evening, they brought [Jesus] many who were possessed by demons, and he drove out the spirits by a word and cured all the sick, to fulfill what had been said by Isaiah the prophet:<br>    "He took away our infirmities<br>      and bore our diseases." |

*Hail Mary*

| | |
|---|---|
| *Psalm 69:10* | Because zeal for your house consumes me,<br>    I am scorned by those who scorn you. |
| *Mark 14:64,65* | [The high priest cried out,] "You have heard the blasphemy. What do you think?" They all condemned [Jesus] as deserving to die. Some began to spit on him. They blindfolded him and struck him and said to him, "Prophesy!" And the guards greeted him with blows. |

*Hail Mary*

| | |
|---|---|
| *Psalm 70:2* | Graciously rescue me, God!<br>    Come quickly to help me, LORD! |
| *John 19:11* | Jesus answered [Pilate], "You would have no power over me if it had not been given to you from above. For this reason the one who handed me over to you has the greater sin." |

*Hail Mary; Glory Be...*
*O My Jesus, forgive us...*

## Reflections:

Dearest Lord Jesus, after asking for Mary's intercession in the Hail Mary's, my thoughts are drawn to how she felt during the scourging. You were "the fruit of her womb," after all, and as a mother a part of her always saw You as her little Baby. And now the soldiers are beating You and ripping Your flesh: flesh that had never known nor deserved such treatment. In fact, those blows were meant for me, as punishment for my sins. I bless You and praise You and ask for forgiveness for the sins I have committed that led You to take this punishment for me. Amen.

Which verse touched your heart? Why?

Was there a time when you received more punishment than you thought you deserved? Have you ever been unreasonable in your retaliation against someone else?

## The Third Sorrowful Mystery:
### The Crowning with Thorns

The Roman soldiers take Jesus to their courtyard and dress him in mock kingly attire, even weaving a "crown" made out of thorns for his head. They bow to him and laugh, and strike him on the head, but Jesus submits to their treatment in silence.

*Fruit of the mystery: moral courage.*

*Our Father*

**Psalm 71:4**     My God, rescue me from the power of the wicked,
                   from the clutches of the violent.

**Matthew 27:27**  Then the soldiers of the governor took Jesus inside the praetorium and gathered the whole cohort around him.

*Hail Mary*

**Psalm 72:9**     May his foes kneel before him,
                   his enemies lick the dust.

**Mark 15:18,19**  [The soldiers] began to salute [Jesus] with, "Hail, King of the Jews!" and kept striking his head with a reed and spitting upon him. They knelt before him in homage.

*Hail Mary*

**Psalm 73:14**    For I am afflicted day after day,
                   chastised every morning.

**Matthew 27:28**  [The soldiers] stripped off [Jesus'] clothes and threw a scarlet military cloak about him.

*Hail Mary*

**Psalm 74:12**    Yet you, God, are my king from of old,
                   winning victories throughout the earth.

**John 18:36,37**  Jesus answered, "My kingdom does not belong to this world... But as it is, my kingdom is not here." So Pilate said to him, "Then you are a king?" Jesus answered, "You say I am a king."

*Hail Mary*

**Psalm 75:8**     But from God who decides,
                   who brings some low and raises others high.

**Matthew 27:24**  Pilate ... took water and washed his hands in the sight of the crowd, saying, "I am innocent of this man's blood. Look to it yourselves."

*Hail Mary*

**Psalm 76:9**    From the heavens you pronounced sentence;
                  the earth was terrified and reduced to silence.

**Matthew 17:5,6**  While [Jesus] was still speaking, behold, a bright cloud cast a
                    shadow over them, then from the cloud came a voice that
                    said, "This is my beloved Son, with whom I am well pleased;
                    listen to him." When the disciples heard this, they fell
                    prostrate and were very much afraid.

*Hail Mary*

**Psalm 77:4**    When I think of God, I groan;
                  as I ponder, my spirit grows faint.

**John 19:7,8**   The Jews answered, "We have a law, and according to that
                  law he ought to die, because he made himself the Son of
                  God." Now when Pilate heard this statement, he became even
                  more afraid.

*Hail Mary*

**Psalm 78:61**   He gave up his might into captivity,
                  his glorious ark into the hands of the foe.

**Matthew 27:29**  Weaving a crown out of thorns, [the soldiers] placed it on
                   [Jesus'] head, and a reed in his right hand. And kneeling
                   before him, they mocked him, saying, "Hail, King of the
                   Jews!"

*Hail Mary*

**Psalm 79:4**    We have become the reproach of our neighbors,
                  the scorn and derision of those around us.

**Matthew 27:30**  [The soldiers] spat upon [Jesus] and took the reed and kept
                   striking him on the head.

*Hail Mary*

**Psalm 80:7-8**  You have left us to be fought over by our neighbors;
                  our enemies deride us.
                  O LORD of hosts, restore us;
                  let your face shine upon us,
                  that we may be saved.

**Matthew 27:31**  And when [the soldiers] had mocked [Jesus], they stripped
                   him of the cloak, dressed him in his own clothes, and led
                   him off to crucify him.

*Hail Mary; Glory Be...*
*O My Jesus, forgive us...*

## Reflections:

My backyard is landscaped, courtesy of the previous owner of our house. There is a small spot by the gate with a row of beautiful but prickly thorn bushes. What struck me today, however, was its half-inch thorns that are needle-sharp and cover the length of the branches. It made me wonder about the Roman soldier who wove the crown of thorns for Jesus' head. How many thorns did the soldier get into his own hands, just to make Jesus suffer? Have I ever had the kind of malice that made me want to hurt someone else, even at the expense of my own well-being? Dearest LORD Jesus, forgive me for such times, just as You forgave the soldier who wove Your crown. Amen.

Which verse touched your heart? Why?

The great irony here is that the cohort is turning the one thing they got right—that Jesus is a king—into a mockery with the crown of thorns. Have you ever made sport of someone's abilities or heritage?

## The Fourth Sorrowful Mystery:
### The Carrying of the Cross

Jesus is made to carry his cross through the streets of Jerusalem to the place of crucifixion, Golgotha.

*Fruit of the mystery: patience.*

### Our Father

| | |
|---|---|
| **Psalm 81:8a** | In distress you called and I rescued you. |
| **Luke 23:42,43** | [The thief] said, "Jesus, remember me when you come into your kingdom." [Jesus] replied to him, "Amen, I say to you, today you will be with me in Paradise." |

### Hail Mary

**Psalm 82:5**    The gods neither know nor understand,
    wandering about in darkness,
    and all the world's foundations shake.

**Matthew 27:45**    Darkness came over the whole land until three in the afternoon.

### Hail Mary

**Psalm 83:3**    See how your enemies rage;
    your foes proudly raise their heads.

**Matthew 27:41**    Likewise the chief priests with the scribes and elders mocked [Jesus].

### Hail Mary

**Psalm 84:3**    My soul yearns and pines
    for the courts of the LORD.
    My heart and flesh cry out
    for the living God.

**Matthew 27:46**    And about three o'clock Jesus cried out in a loud voice, "*Eli, Eli, lema sabachthani?*" which means, "My God, my God, why have you forsaken me?"

### Hail Mary

**Psalm 85:3**    You forgave the guilt of your people,
    pardoned all their sins.

**Luke 23:34**    Then Jesus said, "Father, forgive them, they know not what they do."

### Hail Mary

| | |
|---|---|
| *Psalm 86:14* | O God, the arrogant have risen against me;<br>    a ruthless band has sought my life;<br>    to you they pay no heed. |
| *Matthew 27:44* | The revolutionaries who were crucified with [Jesus] also kept abusing him in the same way. |

*Hail Mary*

| | |
|---|---|
| *Psalm 87:6* | The LORD notes in the register of the peoples:<br>    "This one was born here." |
| *1 Peter 1:3* | Blessed be the God and Father of our Lord Jesus Christ, who in his great mercy gave us a new birth to a living hope through the resurrection of Jesus Christ from the dead. |

*Hail Mary*

| | |
|---|---|
| *Psalm 88:4* | For my soul is filled with troubles;<br>    my life draws near to Sheol. |
| *Matthew 27:50* | But Jesus cried out again in a loud voice, and gave up his spirit. |

*Hail Mary*

| | |
|---|---|
| *Psalm 89:49* | What mortal can live and not see death?<br>    Who can escape the power of Sheol? |
| *John 10:17,18* | [Jesus said,] "This is why the Father loves me, because I lay down my life in order to take it up again. No one takes it from me, but I lay it down on my own. I have power to lay it down, and power to take it up again. This command I have received from my Father." |

*Hail Mary*

| | |
|---|---|
| *Psalm 90:15* | Make us glad as many days as you humbled us,<br>    for as many years as we have seen trouble. |
| *Romans 5:3-5* | Not only that, but we even boast of our afflictions, knowing that affliction produces endurance, and endurance, proven character, and proven character, hope, and hope does not disappoint, because the love of God has been poured out into our hearts through the holy Spirit that has been given to us. |

*Hail Mary; Glory Be...*
*O My Jesus, forgive us...*

## Reflections:

Dearest Lord Jesus, as a carpenter, You were intimately acquainted with wood. You knew how to make chairs, bowls, and many useful things. You had probably even carried big pieces of lumber for some of Your larger jobs. But this time, You were carrying a cross whose only use was for death—Your death. I bless You and praise You and ask for a share in Your acceptance of God's will. Amen.

Which verse touched your heart? Why?

Relate a time when one thing after another seemed to burden you. Compare it to Jesus' betrayal, unjust trial, beating, mockery, and crucifixion.

## The Fifth Sorrowful Mystery:
### The Crucifixion

Jesus, upon the cross, dies for our sins.
*Fruit of the mystery: final perseverance.*

*Our Father*

**Psalm 91:14**     Whoever clings to me, I will deliver;
whoever knows my name I will set on high.
**Luke 23:43**      [Jesus] replied to [the thief], "Amen, I say to you, today you
will be with me in Paradise."

*Hail Mary*

**Psalm 92:6**      How great are your works, LORD!
How profound your purpose!
**Matthew 27:50-52**  But Jesus cried out again in a loud voice, and gave up his
spirit. And behold, the veil of the sanctuary was torn in two
from top to bottom. The earth quaked, rocks were split,
tombs were opened, and the bodies of many saints who had
fallen asleep were raised.

*Hail Mary*

**Psalm 93:2**      Your throne stands firm from of old;
you are from everlasting, LORD.
**John 8:58**       Jesus said to them, "Amen, amen, I say to you, before
Abraham came to be, I AM."

*Hail Mary*

**Psalm 94:17**     If the LORD were not my help,
I would long have been silent in the grave.
**Luke 23:46**      Jesus cried out in a loud voice, "Father, into your hands I
commend my spirit"; and when he had said this he breathed
his last.

*Hail Mary*

**Psalm 95:1**      Come, let us sing joyfully to the LORD;
cry out to the rock of our salvation.
**Romans 5:11**     Not only that, but we also boast of God through our Lord
Jesus Christ, through whom we have now received
reconciliation.

*Hail Mary*

**Psalm 96:2**     Sing to the LORD, bless his name;
                        announce his salvation day after day.
**Acts 2:38**       Peter [said] to [the crowd], "Repent and be baptized, every
                    one of you, in the name of Jesus Christ for the forgiveness
                    of your sins; and you will receive the gift of the holy Spirit."
                            *Hail Mary*

**Psalm 97:10**    The LORD loves those who hate evil,
                        protects the lives of the faithful,
                        rescues them from the hand of the wicked.
**John 19:26,27**  When Jesus saw his mother and the disciple there whom he
                    loved, he said to his mother, "Woman, behold, your son."
                    Then he said to the disciple, "Behold, your mother." And
                    from that hour the disciple took her into his home.
                            *Hail Mary*

**Psalm 98:2**     The LORD has made his victory known;
                        has revealed his triumph for the nations to see.
**Acts 2:23,24**   [Peter said,] "This man, delivered up by the set plan and
                    foreknowledge of God, you killed, using lawless men to
                    crucify him. But God raised him up, releasing him from the
                    throes of death, because it was impossible for him to be held
                    by it."
                            *Hail Mary*

**Psalm 99:8**     O LORD, our God, you answered them;
                        you were a forgiving God,
                        though you punished their offenses.
**John 3:17**      For God did not send his Son into the world to condemn the
                    world, but that the world might be saved through him.
                            *Hail Mary*

**Psalm 100:5**      Good indeed is the LORD,
                    Whose love endures forever,
                        whose faithfulness lasts through every age.
**Revelation 7:11,12** All the angels... prostrated themselves before the throne,
                    worshiped God, and exclaimed:
                        "Amen. Blessing and glory, wisdom and thanksgiving,
                            honor, power, and might
                            be to our God forever and ever. Amen."
                        *Hail Mary; Glory Be...*
                        *O My Jesus, forgive us...*
                        *Hail, Holy Queen*

## Reflections:

Dearest Lord Jesus, thank You so much for Your generosity and mercy and love. You knew from before time began what a weak and sinful person I would turn out to be, and You came to earth to save me. I know, I know,... You came to save everyone else, too—You see how easily I slip into selfishness. I thought that in this mystery through the Psalms I would see the depths of sorrow for the loss of Your earthly life. But all I found was glory and praise at God's great victory and mercy. Thank You for showing me the proper perspective of Your death as a life-giving victory, not a life-taking loss. Amen.

Which verse touched your heart? Why?

Jesus' death made it possible for us to be united to God in a special way, but it was a great sacrifice on His part. Have you ever made a great sacrifice for a loved one?

## The Glorious Mysteries

The Glorious mysteries begin with the Resurrection, in which the apostles discover that Jesus is no longer in His tomb. Jesus visits with the apostles in His resurrected Body. Jesus told his disciples many times before his death that He would rise again. I found it appropriate that in the mystery of the Resurrection, one of the Psalm verses speaks of "his prediction coming to pass".

The Ascension of Jesus into Heaven is the second mystery and chronicles the event when Jesus' resurrected body physically rose into heaven, as the apostles watched in wonder.

The third Glorious mystery, the Descent of the Holy Spirit, relates how the apostles had been waiting in Jerusalem as instructed by Jesus. While they were gathered, the Holy Spirit came down from heaven and came to rest on each of them.

In the fourth mystery of the Assumption of Mary into Heaven, Mary's body and soul are taken to heaven by Jesus. The Catholic Church has not officially defined whether Mary died before she was taken to heaven; however, consider that God had chosen Mary to be without sin even before her birth. "The wages of sin are death," according to the apostle Paul, and since Mary had no sin, it was only just that she should not die.

The final Glorious mystery reveals the Coronation of Mary as Queen of heaven and earth. Mary was not the one who put herself forward; Jesus exalted her with the lavish glory that only a Son who is also God can bestow. His coronation of his Mother is the most perfect fulfillment of the commandment to "honor thy father and thy mother."

## The First Glorious Mystery:
### The Resurrection of the Lord

Jesus is risen from the dead, and is seen by His apostles and followers.
*Fruit of the mystery: faith.*

*Our Father*

*Psalm 101:6*     I look to the faithful of the land;
       they alone can be my companions.
Those who follow the way of integrity,
       they alone can enter my service.

*Matthew 28:9*    And behold, Jesus met [Mary Magdalene and the other Mary] on their way and greeted them. They approached, embraced his feet, and did him homage.

*Hail Mary*

*Psalm 102:14*    You will again show mercy to Zion;
       now is the time for pity;
       the appointed time has come.

*Luke 24:1,3*    But at daybreak on the first day of the week [the women who had come from Galilee with him] took the spices they had prepared and went to the tomb... but when they entered, they did not find the body of the Lord Jesus.

*Hail Mary*

*Psalm 103:4*    [He] delivers your life from the pit,
       surrounds you with love and compassion.

*Luke 24:46,47*    And [Jesus] said to them, "Thus it is written that the Messiah would suffer and rise from the dead on the third day and that repentance, for the forgiveness of sins, would be preached in his name to all the nations."

*Hail Mary*

*Psalm 104:30*    When you send forth your breath, they are created,
       and you renew the face of the earth.

*Luke 24:32*    Then [the disciples] said to each other, "Were not our hearts burning [within us] while he spoke to us on the way and opened the scriptures to us?"

*Hail Mary*

| | |
|---|---|
| **Psalm 105:19** | His prediction came to pass,<br>    and the word of the LORD proved him true. |
| **Luke 24:44,45** | [Jesus] said to them, "These are my words that I spoke to you while I was still with you, that everything written about me in the law of Moses and in the prophets and psalms must be fulfilled." Then he opened their minds to understand the scriptures.<br><div align="center">*Hail Mary*</div> |
| **Psalm 106:5** | That I may see the prosperity of your chosen,<br>    rejoice in the joy of your people,<br>    and glory with your heritage. |
| **Mark 16:17,18** | [Jesus said,] "These signs will accompany those who believe: in my name they will drive out demons, they will speak new languages. They will pick up serpents [with their hands], and if they drink any deadly thing, it will not harm them. They will lay hands on the sick, and they will recover."<br><div align="center">*Hail Mary*</div> |
| **Psalm 107:20,21** | [He] sent forth the word to heal them,<br>    snatched them from the grave.<br>Let them thank the LORD for such kindness,<br>    such wondrous deeds for mere mortals. |
| **Matthew 28:19** | [Jesus said,] "Go, therefore, and make disciples of all nations, baptizing them in the name of the Father, and of the Son, and of the holy Spirit."<br><div align="center">*Hail Mary*</div> |
| **Psalm 108:3** | Awake, my soul; awake, lyre and harp!<br>    I will wake the dawn. |
| **Matthew 28:1** | After the sabbath, as the first day of the week was dawning, Mary Magdalene and the other Mary came to see the tomb.<br><div align="center">*Hail Mary*</div> |
| **Psalm 109:27** | Make them know this is your hand,<br>    that you, LORD, have acted. |
| **Mark 16:6** | [The angel] said to them, "Do not be amazed! You seek Jesus of Nazareth, the crucified. He has been raised; he is not here. Behold the place where they laid him."<br><div align="center">*Hail Mary*</div> |
| **Psalm 110:2** | The scepter of your sovereign might<br>    the LORD will extend from Zion.<br>The LORD says: "Rule over your enemies!" |
| **Matthew 28:18** | Then Jesus approached and said to them, "All power in heaven and on earth has been given to me."<br><div align="center">*Hail Mary; Glory Be...*<br>*O My Jesus, forgive us...*</div> |

## Reflections:

Dearest Lord Jesus, it was not enough for You to die for our sins. You actually overcame death to give us new hope—a higher hope. From that day forward, we had hope: not of a simple earthly happiness, but of a heavenly joy beyond our imagination. I bless You and praise You and thank You for showing us that life does not end with death. Amen.

Which verse touched your heart? Why?

Even though the Crucifixion of Christ was the lowest point of human history, Jesus used it to inaugurate the greatest blessing mankind has ever known. Has there been some event in your life that seemed at first to be bad, but turned out to be an unexpected blessing?

## The Second Glorious Mystery:
### The Ascension of Jesus into Heaven

Jesus rises into heaven and takes his place at the Father's right hand.
*Fruit of the mystery: hope.*

*Our Father*

**Psalm 111:6**   You showed powerful deeds to your people,
        giving them the lands of the nations.

**John 20:30,31**   Now Jesus did many other signs in the presence of [his] disciples that are not written in this book. But these are written that you may [come to] believe that Jesus is the Messiah, the Son of God, and that through this belief you may have life in his name.

*Hail Mary*

**Psalm 112:4**   They shine through the darkness, a light for the upright;
        they are gracious, merciful, and just.

**John 12:35,36**   Jesus said to them, "...Walk while you have the light, so that darkness may not overcome you. Whoever walks in the dark does not know where he is going. While you have the light, believe in the light, so that you may become children of the light."

*Hail Mary*

**Psalm 113:5,6**   Who is like the LORD,
        our God enthroned on high,
        looking down on heaven and earth?

**Mark16:19**   So then the Lord Jesus, after he spoke to them, was taken up into heaven and took his seat at the right hand of God.

*Hail Mary*

**Psalm 114:7**   Tremble, earth, before the Lord,
        before the God of Jacob.

**Revelation 1:12-17**   Then I turned to see whose voice it was that spoke to me, and when I turned, I saw... one like a son of man,...
        When I caught sight of him, I fell down at his feet as though dead. He touched me with his right hand and said, "Do not be afraid. I am the first and the last."

*Hail Mary*

**Psalm 115:1**   Not to us, LORD, not to us
        but to your name give glory
        because of your faithfulness and love.

**Philippians 2:9**   Because of this, God greatly exalted [Jesus]
        and bestowed on him the name
        that is above every name.

*Hail Mary*

| | |
|---|---|
| *Psalm 116:9* | I shall walk before the LORD<br>    in the land of the living. |
| *John 11:25-27* | Jesus told [Martha], "I am the resurrection and the life... Do you believe this?" She said to him, "Yes, Lord. I have come to believe." |

*Hail Mary*

| | |
|---|---|
| *Psalm 117:1,2* | Praise the LORD, all you nations!<br>    Give glory, all you peoples!<br>The LORD's love for us is strong;<br>    the LORD is faithful forever.<br>Hallelujah! |
| *Acts 2:38,39* | Peter [said] to them, "Repent and be baptized, every one of you, ... For the promise is made to you and to your children and to all those far off, whomever the Lord our God will call." |

*Hail Mary*

| | |
|---|---|
| *Psalm 118:19* | Open the gates of victory;<br>    I will enter and thank the LORD. |
| *Hebrews 12:2* | For the sake of the joy that lay before him [Jesus] endured the cross, despising its shame, and has taken his seat at the right of the throne of God. |

*Hail Mary*

| | |
|---|---|
| *Psalm 119:89* | Your word, LORD, stands forever;<br>    it is firm as the heavens. |
| *John 1:1,2* | In the beginning was the Word,<br>    and the Word was with God,<br>    and the Word was God.<br>He was in the beginning with God. |

*Hail Mary*

| | |
|---|---|
| *Psalm 120:6* | Too long did I live<br>    among those who hated peace. |
| *John 20:19* | On the evening of that first day of the week, when the doors were locked, where the disciples were, for fear of the Jews, Jesus came and stood in their midst and said to them, "Peace be with you." |

*Hail Mary; Glory Be...*
*O My Jesus, forgive us...*

## Reflections:

Jesus had changed the lives of the Apostles in so many ways. He had brought them to a new, radical way of understanding Who God is. And then there was Mary. How did Mary say good-bye as Jesus rose to Heaven that Thursday? Luke's account doesn't say. What Luke does say is that all were filled with hope.

Which verse touched your heart? Why?

Why would the idea of Jesus "leaving" fill us with hope today?

## The Third Glorious Mystery:
# The Descent of the Holy Spirit

During the Jewish feast of Pentecost, or Fifty Days, all the Jews assemble in Jerusalem (as at Passover). This is also the time when Jesus sends the Holy Spirit upon the apostles to begin their ministry to the world.

*Fruit of the mystery: love of God.*

### Our Father

| | |
|---|---|
| *Psalm 121:5* | The LORD is your guardian; |
| | the LORD is your shade |
| | at your right hand. |
| *Acts 2:36* | [Peter said,] "Therefore let the whole house of Israel know for certain that God has made him both Lord and Messiah, this Jesus whom you crucified." |

### Hail Mary

| | |
|---|---|
| *Psalm 122:4* | [To Jerusalem] the tribes have come, |
| | the tribes of the LORD, |
| | As it was decreed for Israel, |
| | to give thanks to the name of the LORD. |
| *Acts 2:1,5* | When the time for Pentecost was fulfilled... there were devout Jews from every nation under heaven staying in Jerusalem. |

### Hail Mary

| | |
|---|---|
| *Psalm 123:1* | To you I raise my eyes, |
| | to you enthroned in heaven. |
| *Mark 16:19* | So then the Lord Jesus,... was taken up into heaven and took his seat at the right hand of God. |

### Hail Mary

| | |
|---|---|
| *Psalm 124:8* | Our help is in the name of the LORD, |
| | the maker of heaven and earth. |
| *Acts 17:24,25* | The God who made the world and all that is in it, the Lord of heaven and earth,... [he] gives to everyone life and breath and everything. |

### Hail Mary

| | |
|---|---|
| *Psalm 125:2* | As mountains surround Jerusalem, |
| | the LORD surrounds his people |
| | both now and forever. |
| *Acts 2:17* | "It will come to pass in the last days," God says, |
| | "that I will pour out a portion of my spirit |
| | upon all flesh. |
| | Your sons and your daughters shall prophesy, |
| | your young men shall see visions, |
| | your old men shall dream dreams." |

### Hail Mary

| | |
|---|---|
| *Psalm 126:2* | Our mouths were filled with laughter;<br>    our tongues sang for joy.<br>Then it was said among the nations,<br>    "The LORD has done great things for them." |
| *Acts 2:4* | And [the apostles] were all filled with the holy Spirit and began to speak in different tongues, as the Spirit enabled them to proclaim. |

*Hail Mary*

| | |
|---|---|
| *Psalm 127:1* | Unless the LORD build the house,<br>    they labor in vain who build.<br>Unless the LORD guard the city,<br>    in vain does the guard keep watch. |
| *Acts 2:2* | And suddenly there came from the sky a noise like a strong driving wind, and it filled the entire house in which [the apostles] were. |

*Hail Mary*

| | |
|---|---|
| *Psalm 128:4* | Just so will they be blessed<br>    who fear the LORD. |
| *Acts 1:8* | [Jesus said,] "But you will receive power when the holy Spirit comes upon you, and you will be my witnesses in Jerusalem, throughout Judea and Samaria, and to the ends of the earth." |

*Hail Mary*

| | |
|---|---|
| *Psalm 129:2* | Much have they oppressed me from my youth,<br>    yet they have not prevailed. |
| *Romans 8:18* | I consider that the sufferings of this present time are as nothing compared with the glory to be revealed for us. |

*Hail Mary*

| | |
|---|---|
| *Psalm 130:7* | Let Israel look for the LORD,<br>For with the LORD is kindness,<br>    with him is full redemption. |
| *Romans 9:6,15* | But it is not that the word of God has failed. For not all who are of Israel are Israel,... For he says to Moses:<br>"I will show mercy to whom I will,<br>    I will take pity on whom I will." |

*Hail Mary; Glory Be...*
*O My Jesus, forgive us...*

## Reflections:

We are called to come together as a community. Together, we receive the gift of the Holy Spirit: now it's "Go time." The Apostles, in an earlier part of their lives, said "yes" to following and learning from Jesus. Now, they're being called to "do"; to "accomplish"… for the rest of their lives. We who follow after them are called to do the same.

Which verse touched your heart? Why?

I've been called to follow… to learn… and to act. How am I doing in *each* of these categories?

## The Fourth Glorious Mystery:
### The Assumption of Mary into Heaven

When Mary grew old, her body was taken by God into heaven. All who have faith in Christ have the promise to share in the resurrection of the body, but Mary was taken first as a gesture of love from a Son to His Mother.
*Fruit of the mystery: greater devotion to Mary.*

*Our Father*

| | |
|---|---|
| *Psalm 131:1* | LORD, my heart is not proud; <br> nor are my eyes haughty. <br> I do not busy myself with great matters, <br> with things too sublime for me. |
| *Romans 12:12* | Rejoice in hope, endure in affliction, persevere in prayer. |

*Hail Mary*

| | |
|---|---|
| *Psalm 132:14* | "This is my resting place forever; <br> here will I dwell, for I desire it." |
| *John 10:28* | [Jesus said,] "I give them eternal life, and they shall never perish. No one can take them out of my hand." |

*Hail Mary*

| | |
|---|---|
| *Psalm 133:1* | How good it is, how pleasant, <br> where the people dwell as one! |
| *Romans 1:11,12* | For I long to see you, that I may share with you some spiritual gift so that you may be strengthened, that is, that you and I may be mutually encouraged by one another's faith, yours and mine. |

*Hail Mary*

| | |
|---|---|
| *Psalm 134:1* | Come, bless the LORD, <br> all you servants of the LORD <br> Who stand in the house of the LORD <br> through the long hours of night. |
| *John 12:26* | [Jesus said,] "Whoever serves me must follow me, and where I am, there also will my servant be. The Father will honor whoever serves me." |

*Hail Mary*

| | |
|---|---|
| *Psalm 135:6* | Whatever the LORD wishes <br> he does in heaven and on earth, <br> in the seas and in all the deeps. |
| *Philippians 3:20,21* | But our citizenship is in heaven, and from it we also await a savior, the Lord Jesus Christ. He will change our lowly body to conform with his glorified body by the power that enables him also to bring all things into subjection to himself. |

*Hail Mary*

| | |
|---|---|
| *Psalm 136:26* | Praise the God of heaven,<br>God's love endures forever. |
| *Ephesians 2:4-7* | But God, who is rich in mercy, because of the great love he had for us, even when we were dead in our transgressions, brought us to life with Christ (by grace you have been saved), raised us up with him, and seated us with him in the heavens in Christ Jesus. |

*Hail Mary*

| | |
|---|---|
| *Psalm 137:4* | But how could we sing a song of the LORD<br>in a foreign land? |
| *Ephesians 2:19* | So then you are no longer strangers and sojourners, but you are fellow citizens with the holy ones and members of the household of God. |

*Hail Mary*

| | |
|---|---|
| *Psalm 138:8* | The LORD is with me to the end.<br>LORD, your love endures forever.<br>Never forsake the work of your hands! |
| *Acts 2:27* | Because you will not abandon my soul to the nether world, nor will you suffer your holy one to see corruption. |

*Hail Mary*

| | |
|---|---|
| *Psalm 139:14* | I praise you, so wonderfully you made me;<br>wonderful are your works!<br>My very self you knew. |
| *1 Corinthians 15:22,23* | For just as in Adam all die, so too in Christ shall all be brought to life, but each one in proper order. |

*Hail Mary*

| | |
|---|---|
| *Psalm 140:14* | Then the just will give thanks to your name;<br>the upright will dwell in your presence. |
| *Acts 2:28* | You have made known to me the paths of life;<br>you will fill me with joy in your presence. |

*Hail Mary; Glory Be...*
*O My Jesus, forgive us...*

## Reflections:

When Jesus suffered, Mary – a mother attuned to her child – also suffered. Jesus was lost as a teenager for three days. Later in life, He was savagely beaten. Spikes were driven through His hands (wrists) and feet. He was crucified. His side was sliced open. By earthly accounts, we should feel nothing but pity for both Jesus and Mary. And yet, we feel inspired ... because Mary's acceptance of her suffering transcends earthly understanding. She was perfectly "of God" in every moment of her life. Other than God Himself in the person of Jesus Christ, no holier, no better, no more perfect example of how to live will ever exist for us.

Which verse touched your heart? Why?

Down deep, as far inside my heart and soul as I can get, do I really want to become more like Mary, more like Christ? What can I point to specifically in the last two weeks to show this? What will I be able to point to today to show this?

## The Fifth Glorious Mystery:
### The Coronation of Mary as Queen of Heaven

In the Old Testament, some kings had more than one wife. Wise King Solomon instituted his mother as "queen" to avoid undue strain among his wives. Jesus is King in heaven, and crowns his Mother as his Queen.

*Fruit of the mystery: eternal happiness.*

### Our Father

| | |
|---|---|
| **Psalm 141:2** | Let my prayer be incense before you; my uplifted hands an evening sacrifice. |
| **Romans 12:1** | I urge you therefore, brothers, by the mercies of God, to offer your bodies as a living sacrifice, holy and pleasing to God, your spiritual worship. |

### Hail Mary

| | |
|---|---|
| **Psalm 142:8** | Lead me out of my prison, that I may give thanks to your name. Then the just shall gather around me because you have been good to me. |
| **Hebrews 12:1** | Therefore, since we are surrounded by so great a cloud of witnesses, let us rid ourselves of every burden... and persevere in running the race that lies before us. |

### Hail Mary

| | |
|---|---|
| **Psalm 143:10** | Teach me to do your will, for you are my God. May your kind spirit guide me on ground that is level. |
| **John 14:26** | The Advocate, the holy Spirit that the Father will send in my name—he will teach you everything and remind you of all that [I] told you. |

### Hail Mary

| | |
|---|---|
| **Psalm 144:15** | Happy the people so blessed; happy the people whose God is the LORD. |
| **John 14:1-3** | [Jesus told his apostles,] "Do not let your hearts be troubled... if I go and prepare a place for you, I will come back again and take you to myself, so that where I am you also may be." |

### Hail Mary

**Psalm 145:13a**   Your reign is a reign for all ages,
 your dominion for all generations.
**Revelation 7:11,12**  All the angels... worshiped God, and exclaimed:
 "Amen. Blessing and glory, wisdom and thanksgiving,
 honor, power, and might
 be to our God forever and ever. Amen."
 *Hail Mary*

**Psalm 146:2**   Praise the LORD, my soul;
 I shall praise the LORD all my life,
 sing praise to my God while I live.
**1 Thessalonians 5:9,10**   For God did not destine us for wrath, but to gain
 salvation through our Lord Jesus Christ, who died for us, so
 that whether we are awake or asleep we may live together
 with him.
 *Hail Mary*

**Psalm 147:11**   Rather the LORD takes pleasure in the devout,
 those who await his faithful care.
**James 1:12**   Blessed is the man who perseveres in temptation, for when
 he has been proved he will receive the crown of life.
 *Hail Mary*

**Psalm 148:13**   Let them all praise the LORD's name,
 for his name alone is exalted,
 majestic above earth and heaven.
**Romans 11:36**   For from him and through him and for him are all things. To
 him be glory forever.
 *Hail Mary*

**Psalm 149:4**   For the LORD takes delight in his people,
 honors the poor with victory.
**2 Timothy 4:7-8a**  I have competed well; I have finished the race; I have kept
 the faith. From now on the crown of righteousness awaits
 me.
 *Hail Mary*

**Psalm 150:2**   Give praise for his mighty deeds,
 praise him for his great majesty.
**Revelation 5:13**   Then I heard... everything in the universe, cry out:
 "To the one who sits on the throne and to the Lamb
 be blessing and honor, glory and might,
 forever and ever."
 *Hail Mary;  Glory Be...*
 *O My Jesus, forgive us...*
 *Hail, Holy Queen*

## Reflections:

This is the only mystery that occurs in Heaven. And there's a reason why. Every mystery of each decade of the rosary serves to separate us from the secular; the "earthly". We are to focus on wisdom, knowledge, and example. In this, the last Glorious mystery, we see what our goal truly is: eternal Happiness in Heaven, united with God the Father, Jesus, the Holy Spirit.... as well as the Queen of Heaven... Mary.

Which verse touched your heart? Why?

Am I living my life as if Mary can help me obtain eternal happiness? Am I willing to ask her to help me, right here; right now?

## The Luminous Mysteries

The Luminous mysteries involve the life of Jesus during His public ministry. The first is the baptism of Jesus by John the Baptist in the river Jordan, where Jesus is first revealed as God's Son.

Jesus' first public miracle, changing water into wine at the wedding feast of Cana, is the second Luminous mystery.

The third mystery is not so much one event as his entire period spent on the proclamation of the kingdom of God.

Jesus went with Peter, James and John to the top of Mount Tabor, where the disciples received a vision of Christ in His glory. This event is known as the Transfiguration and makes up the fourth mystery.

The final mystery is the Institution of the Holy Eucharist at the Last Supper the night before Jesus' death.

*Apostle's Creed*
*Our Father; 3 Hail Marys; Glory Be*

## The First Luminous Mystery:
### The Baptism of the Lord

Jesus goes to John the Baptist at the River Jordan and is baptized by John.
*Fruit of the mystery: openness to the Holy Spirit*

*Our Father*

| | |
|---|---|
| **Sirach 1:4** | Before all things else wisdom was created; |
| | and prudent understanding, from eternity. |
| **John 1:1,14** | In the beginning was the Word, |
| | and the Word was with God, |
| | and the Word was God... |
| | And the Word became flesh |
| | and made his dwelling among us, |
| | and we saw his glory, |
| | the glory as of the Father's only Son, |
| | full of grace and truth. |

*Hail Mary*

| | |
|---|---|
| **Sirach 2:6** | Trust God and he will help you; |
| | make straight your ways and hope in him. |
| **Luke 3:3,4** | [John] went throughout [the] whole region of the Jordan, proclaiming a baptism of repentance for the forgiveness of sins, as it is written in the book of the words of the prophet Isaiah: |
| | "A voice of one crying out in the desert: |
| | 'Prepare the way of the Lord, |
| | make straight his paths.'" |

*Hail Mary*

| | |
|---|---|
| **Sirach 3:18** | Humble yourself the more, the greater you are, |
| | and you will find favor with God. |
| **Matthew 3:13** | Then Jesus came from Galilee to John at the Jordan to be baptized by him. |

*Hail Mary*

| | |
|---|---|
| **Sirach 4:23** | Refrain not from speaking at the proper time, |
| | and hide not away your wisdom. |
| **John 1:29** | The next day [John] saw Jesus coming toward him and said, "Behold, the Lamb of God, who takes away the sin of the world." |

*Hail Mary*

| | |
|---|---|
| *Sirach 5:8* | Delay not your conversion to the LORD,<br>   put it not off from day to day. |
| *Matthew 3:2,8* | [John the Baptist said,] "Repent, for the kingdom of heaven is at hand! Produce good fruit as evidence of your repentance." |

*Hail Mary*

| | |
|---|---|
| *Sirach 6:17* | For he who fears God behaves accordingly,<br>   and his friend will be like himself. |
| *Mark 1:7,8* | And this is what [John] proclaimed: "One mightier than I is coming after me. I am not worthy to stoop and loosen the thongs of his sandals. I have baptized you with water; he will baptize you with the holy Spirit." |

*Hail Mary*

| | |
|---|---|
| *Sirach 7:30* | With all your strength, love your Creator,<br>   forsake not his ministers. |
| *Matthew 3:14,15* | John tried to prevent [Jesus], saying, "I need to be baptized by you, and yet you are coming to me?" Jesus said to him in reply, "Allow it now, for thus it is fitting for us to fulfill all righteousness." Then he allowed him. |

*Hail Mary*

| | |
|---|---|
| *Sirach 8:8* | Spurn not the discourse of the wise,<br>   but acquaint yourself with their proverbs;<br>From them you will acquire the training<br>   to serve in the presence of princes. |
| *Luke 3:10* | And the crowds asked [John], "What then should we do?" |

*Hail Mary*

| | |
|---|---|
| *Sirach 9:15* | With the learned be intimate;<br>   let all your conversation be about the law of the LORD. |
| *Mark 1:8,9* | [John the Baptist said,] "I have baptized you with water; he will baptize you with the holy Spirit."<br>   It happened in those days that Jesus came from Nazareth of Galilee and was baptized in the Jordan by John. |

*Hail Mary*

| | |
|---|---|
| *Sirach 10:27* | My son, with humility have self-esteem;<br>   prize yourself as you deserve. |
| *Matthew 3:16,17* | After Jesus was baptized, he came up from the water and behold, the heavens were opened [for him], and he saw the Spirit of God descending like a dove [and] coming upon him. And a voice came from the heavens, saying, "This is my beloved Son, with whom I am well pleased." |

*Hail Mary; Glory Be...*
*O My Jesus, forgive us...*

## Reflections:

Jesus met every standard for Jewish piety. From the timing of His Birth and being presented to God His Father in the Temple, to following Jewish traditions and devotional practices such as the annual pilgrimage to Jerusalem for Passover. He even undertook the symbolic baptism of repentance. Jesus did everything just the right way.

Which verse touched your heart? Why?

Is there an area of your life in which you could be more diligent?

## The Second Luminous Mystery:
### The Miracle of Cana

Mary, Jesus, and his followers are invited to a wedding in Cana. During the festivities afterward, the wedding couple runs out of wine for their guests. Mary goes to Jesus and tells him of the problem. Jesus turns water into wine.
*Fruit of the mystery: to Jesus through Mary*

### Our Father

| | |
|---|---|
| **Sirach 11:22** | God's blessing is the lot of the just man, and in due time his hopes bear fruit. |
| **John 2:1a,2** | On the third day there was a wedding in Cana in Galilee... Jesus and his disciples were ... invited to the wedding. |

### Hail Mary

| | |
|---|---|
| **Sirach 12:1** | If you do good, know for whom you are doing it, and your kindness will have its effect. |
| **John 2:3** | When the wine ran short, the mother of Jesus said to [Jesus], "They have no wine." |

### Hail Mary

| | |
|---|---|
| **Sirach 13:10** | Be not bold with [a man of influence] lest you be rebuffed, but keep not too far away lest you be forgotten. |
| **John 2:4** | Jesus said to [his mother], "Woman, how does your concern affect me? My hour has not yet come." |

### Hail Mary

| | |
|---|---|
| **Sirach 14:13** | Before you die, be good to your friend, and give him a share in what you possess. |
| **John 2:5** | His mother said to the servers, "Do whatever he tells you." |

### Hail Mary

| | |
|---|---|
| **Sirach 15:19** | The eyes of God see all he has made; he understands man's every deed. |
| **John 2:6,7** | Now there were six stone water jars there for Jewish ceremonial washings, each holding twenty to thirty gallons. Jesus told [the servants], "Fill the jars with water." So they filled them to the brim. |

### Hail Mary

| | |
|---|---|
| **Sirach 16:27** | Then the LORD looked upon the earth, and filled it with his blessings. |
| **John 2:8** | Then [Jesus] told them, "Draw some out now and take it to the headwaiter." So they took it. |

### Hail Mary

| | |
|---|---|
| *Sirach 17:11* | His majestic glory their eyes beheld,<br>        his glorious voice their ears heard. |
| *John 2:11* | Jesus did this as the beginning of his signs in Cana in Galilee and so revealed his glory, and his disciples began to believe in him. |

*Hail Mary*

| | |
|---|---|
| *Sirach 18:2* | Whom has he made equal to describing his works,<br>        and who can probe his mighty deeds? |
| *John 2:9* | And when the headwaiter tasted the water that had become wine, without knowing where it came from (although the servers who had drawn the water knew), the headwaiter called the bridegroom. |

*Hail Mary*

| | |
|---|---|
| *Sirach 19:7* | Tell nothing to friend or foe;<br>        if you have a fault, reveal it not. |
| *John 2:9b-10a* | The headwaiter called the bridegroom and said to him, "Everyone serves good wine first, and then when people have drunk freely, an inferior one." |

*Hail Mary*

| | |
|---|---|
| *Sirach 20:8* | Some misfortunes bring success;<br>        some things gained are a man's loss. |
| *John 2:10b* | [The headwaiter called the bridegroom and said to him,] "You have kept the good wine until now." |

*Hail Mary; Glory Be...*
*O My Jesus, forgive us...*

**Reflections:**

One of the last phrases in the Hail Mary is "pray for us sinners now." Just as the groom and bride needed Jesus' help at their wedding feast, we need Jesus' help in our lives today. And sometimes, just like that couple in Cana, we don't even realize that Jesus is the One who can avert disaster. Thankfully, His mother Mary does know that Jesus can help each situation, and is ready to intercede on our behalf.

Which verse touched your heart? Why?

.

Name a time when the Lord helped you without your first asking for help.

## The Third Luminous Mystery:
## **The Proclamation of the Kingdom of God**

Jesus spends three years going from place to place, telling people of God's love for everyone, God's will for our lives, and God's willingness to help us live for Him.

*Fruit of the mystery: repentance and trust in God*

**Our Father**

**Sirach 21:13**  A wise man's knowledge wells up in a flood,
        and his counsel, like a living spring.

**John 4:14**  [Jesus told the Samaritan woman,] "Whoever drinks the water I shall give will never thirst; the water I shall give will become in him a spring of water welling up to eternal life."

**Hail Mary**

**Sirach 22:17**  A resolve that is backed by prudent understanding
        is like the polished surface of a smooth wall.

**Mark 12:34**  And when Jesus saw that [the scribe] answered with understanding, he said to him, "You are not far from the kingdom of God."

**Hail Mary**

**Sirach 23:27**  Thus all who dwell on the earth shall know,
        and all who inhabit the world shall understand,
That nothing is better than the fear of the LORD,
        nothing more salutary than to obey his commandments.

**Matthew 22:37,38**  [Jesus said to the scribe], "You shall love the Lord, your God, with all your heart, with all your soul, and with all your mind. This is the greatest and the first commandment."

**Hail Mary**

**Sirach 24:21**  He who obeys me will not be put to shame;
        he who serves me will never fail.

**Matthew 5:11,12**  [Jesus told the crowd,] "Blessed are you when they insult you and persecute you and utter every kind of evil against you [falsely] because of me. Rejoice and be glad, for your reward will be great in heaven."

**Hail Mary**

**Sirach 25:1**  With three things I am delighted,
        for they are pleasing to the LORD and to men:
Harmony among brethren, friendship among neighbors,
        and the mutual love of husband and wife.

**Matthew 19:4-6**  [Jesus] said in reply, "Have you not read that from the beginning the Creator 'made them male and female' and said, 'For this reason a man shall leave his father and mother and be joined to his wife, and the two shall become one flesh'? So they are no longer two, but one flesh. Therefore, what God has joined together, no human being must separate."

*Hail Mary*

**Sirach 26:4**  [The man who fears the Lord,] be he rich or poor, his
heart is content,
and a smile is ever on his face.
**Matthew 11:28-30**  [Jesus said,] "Come to me, all you who labor and are burdened, and I will give you rest. Take my yoke upon you and learn from me, for I am meek and humble of heart; and you will find rest for your selves. For my yoke is easy, and my burden light."

*Hail Mary*

**Sirach 27:6**  The fruit of a tree shows the care it has had;
so too does a man's speech disclose the bent of his mind.
**Matthew 7:16,17**  [Jesus said,] "By their fruits you will know them. Do people pick grapes from thorn bushes, or figs from thistles? Just so, every good tree bears good fruit, and a rotten tree bears bad fruit."

*Hail Mary*

**Sirach 28:7**  Think of the commandments, hate not your neighbor;
[think] of the Most High's covenant, and overlook faults.
**Matthew 7:12**  [Jesus said,] "Do to others whatever you would have them do to you. This is the law and the prophets."

*Hail Mary*

**Sirach 29:11**  Dispose of your treasure as the Most High commands,
for that will profit you more than the gold.
**Luke 12:33**  [Jesus told his disciples,] "Sell your belongings and give alms. Provide money bags for yourselves that do not wear out, an inexhaustible treasure in heaven that no thief can reach nor moth destroy."

*Hail Mary*

**Sirach 30:4**  At [his] death, he will seem not dead,
since he leaves after him one like himself.
**John 16:13**  [Jesus said,] "But when he comes, the Spirit of truth, he will guide you to all truth. He will not speak on his own, but he will speak what he hears, and will declare to you the things that are coming."

*Hail Mary; Glory Be...*
*O My Jesus, forgive us...*

## Reflections:

The evangelist John tells us that recording every word spoken by Jesus was not possible at that time; but he also tells us that what was preserved is enough for us to come to the decision of faith in Jesus Christ as God's Son.

Jesus never shied away from a difficult topic, nor did he refuse a sincere request for knowledge. Difficult topics were rarely settled to His listeners' liking, and those who sought to trick Him with clever questions were taken aback by answers that were more clever by far. Even so, Jesus was always teaching, always giving us insight into His thoughts and attitudes.

Which verse touched your heart? Why?

The words we choose to say or not to say, our intonation, all of these reflect who we are. Recall a time when something you said revealed much more about yourself than you were ready to divulge.

## The Fourth Luminous Mystery:
## **The Transfiguration**

Jesus takes Peter, James and John to the top of Mount Tabor. While there, Jesus becomes dazzling white and shows His glory to Peter, James and John.

*Fruit of the mystery: desire for holiness*

### *Our Father*

*Sirach 31:9a,10*  Who is he, that we may praise him?
He, of all his kindred, has done wonders, ...
  and this remains his glory;
He could have sinned but did not,
  could have done evil but would not.

*Luke 9:29*  While [Jesus] was praying his face changed in appearance and his clothing became dazzling white.

### *Hail Mary*

*Sirach 32:13*  Above all, give praise to your Creator,
  who showers his favors upon you.

*Luke 9:32*  Peter and his companions had been overcome by sleep, but becoming fully awake, they saw [Jesus'] glory and the two men standing with him.

### *Hail Mary*

*Sirach 33:13*  Like clay in the hands of a potter,
  to be molded according to his pleasure,
So are men in the hands of their Creator,
  to be assigned by him their function.

*Luke 9:34,35*  While [Jesus] was still speaking, a cloud came and cast a shadow over them, and they became frightened when they entered the cloud. Then from the cloud came a voice that said, "This is my chosen Son; listen to him."

### *Hail Mary*

*Sirach 34:13*  Lively is the courage of those who fear the LORD,
  for they put their hope in their savior.

*Luke 9:33*  As they were about to part from him, Peter said to Jesus, "Master, it is good that we are here; let us make three tents, one for you, one for Moses, and one for Elijah." But he did not know what he was saying.

### *Hail Mary*

*Sirach 35:16*  He who serves God willingly is heard;
  his petition reaches the heavens.

*Luke 9:35*  Then from the cloud came a voice that said, "This is my chosen Son; listen to him."

### *Hail Mary*

*Sirach 36:15-17*    Reward those who have hoped in you,
          and let your prophets be proved true.
      Hear the prayer of your servants,
          for you are ever gracious to your people;
      Thus it will be known to the very ends of the earth
          that you are the eternal God.

*Matthew 17:5*    While [Jesus] was still speaking, behold, a bright cloud cast a shadow over them, then from the cloud came a voice that said, "This is my beloved Son, with whom I am well pleased; listen to him."

*Hail Mary*

*Sirach 37:15*    Most important of all, pray to God
          to set your feet in the path of truth.

*Matthew 17:7*    But Jesus came and touched them, saying, "Rise, and do not be afraid."

*Hail Mary*

*Sirach 38:8*    Thus God's creative work continues without cease
          in its efficacy on the surface of the earth.

*Luke 9:37*    On the next day, when [Jesus and the three disciples] came down from the mountain, a large crowd met him.

*Hail Mary*

*Sirach 39:9*    Many will praise his understanding;
          his fame can never be effaced;
      Unfading will be his memory,
          through all generations his name will live.

*Matthew 17:3*    And behold, Moses and Elijah appeared to them, conversing with [Jesus].

*Hail Mary*

*Sirach 40:17*    But goodness will never be cut off,
          and justice endures forever.
      Wealth or wages can make life sweet,
          but better than either is finding a treasure.

*1 Peter 1:7*    The genuineness of your faith, more precious than gold that is perishable even though tested by fire, may prove to be for praise, glory, and honor at the revelation of Jesus Christ.

*Hail Mary; Glory Be...*
*O My Jesus, forgive us...*

## Reflections:

The last line of the Hail Mary states "pray for us sinners, now and at the hour of our death." There are only two times in our lives that really matter: the present moment ("now"), and the moment of judgment when we encounter Jesus in His glory ("at the hour of our death"). Mary intercedes for us at both times.

Which verse touched your heart? Why?

How often do we ask others for help: in relationships, in physical exertion, in mental calculations? Should we be asking for more help in our spiritual lives?

## The Fifth Luminous Mystery:
### The Institution of the Holy Eucharist

At the Last Supper, Jesus takes bread and wine and turns them into His Body and Blood, so that we can share in His life with Him for all ages.
*Fruit of the mystery: adoration*

### Our Father

| | |
|---|---|
| *Sirach 41:11* | Man's body is a fleeting thing, <br> but a virtuous name will never be annihilated. |
| *Mark 14:9* | [Jesus said,] "Amen, I say to you, wherever the gospel is proclaimed to the whole world, what she has done will be told in memory of her." |

### Hail Mary

| | |
|---|---|
| *Sirach 42:15* | Now will I recall God's works; <br> what I have seen, I will describe. <br> At God's word were his works brought into being; <br> they do his will as he has ordained for them. |
| *1 Corinthians 11:23* | I received from the Lord what I also handed on to you, that the Lord Jesus, on the night he was handed over, took bread. |

### Hail Mary

| | |
|---|---|
| *Sirach 43:35* | It is the LORD who has made all things, <br> and to those who fear him he gives wisdom. |
| *John 6:57* | [Jesus said,] "Just as the living Father sent me and I have life because of the Father, so also the one who feeds on me will have life because of me." |

### Hail Mary

| | |
|---|---|
| *Sirach 44:20a* | He observed the precepts of the Most High, <br> and entered into an agreement with him. |
| *Luke 22:13-14* | Then [the apostles] went off and found everything exactly as [Jesus] had told them, and there they prepared the Passover. <br> When the hour came, he took his place at table with the apostles. |

### Hail Mary

| | |
|---|---|
| *Sirach 45:7* | He made him perpetual in his office <br> when he bestowed on him the priesthood of his people; <br> He established him in honor <br> and crowned him with lofty majesty. |
| *1 Corinthians 11:25b* | [Jesus said,] "Do this, as often as you drink it, in remembrance of me." |

### Hail Mary

**Sirach 46:13a**   Beloved of his people, dear to his Maker,
        dedicated from his mother's womb,
        Consecrated to the LORD.
**Matthew 3:16,17**   After Jesus was baptized, ...a voice came from the heavens, saying, "This is my beloved Son, with whom I am well pleased."

*Hail Mary*

**Sirach 47:22**   But God does not withdraw his mercy,
        nor permit even one of his promises to fail.
He does not uproot the posterity of his chosen one,
        nor destroy the offspring of his friend.
So he gave to Jacob a remnant,
        to David a root from his own family.
**Mark 10:47**   On hearing that it was Jesus of Nazareth, [Bartimaeus] began to cry out and say, "Jesus, son of David, have pity on me."

*Hail Mary*

**Sirach 48:11**   Blessed is he who shall have seen you before he dies.
**Luke 23:42-43**   Then [the criminal] said, "Jesus, remember me when you come into your kingdom." He replied to him, "Amen, I say to you, today you will be with me in Paradise."

*Hail Mary*

**Sirach 49:3**   He turned to God with his whole heart,
        and, though times were evil, he practiced virtue.
**Hebrews 4:15**   For we do not have a high priest who is unable to sympathize with our weaknesses, but one who has similarly been tested in every way, yet without sin.

*Hail Mary*

**Sirach 50:19**   All the people of the land would shout for joy,
        praying to the Merciful One,
As the high priest completed the services at the altar
        by presenting to God the sacrifice due.
**Luke 23:47**   The centurion who witnessed what had happened glorified God and said, "This man was innocent beyond doubt."

*Hail Mary; Glory Be...*
*O My Jesus, forgive us...*
*Hail, Holy Queen*

# Reflections:

During the Catholic liturgy, any one of four "Eucharistic Prayers" may be used for the consecration. The priest says the words of Christ, "This is My body," and, "This is My blood" - and Christ's words become effective once again to turn plain bread and wine into the flesh and blood of Jesus. Each prayer recites a Gospel account of the Last Supper, or the account from Corinthians. Each begins slightly differently, to place emphasis on different things.

† [Prayer I] "On the day before He suffered... He gave You thanks and praise": While listening to the parts of the Mass, this phrase took my breath away. Jesus knew what He would soon endure, and yet He gave God thanks— and praise!! I just could not fathom this. Then I realized that Jesus was looking beyond the pain of the Cross to His victory over sin and death. How childish I am in my short-sightedness.

† [Prayer II] "Before He was given up to death, a death He freely accepted": Notice that the wording of this passage was very carefully chosen. Jesus was not "killed;" He was "given up to death." In fact, the next line states clearly that His death was "freely accepted." No one could take Jesus' life unless He gave it; and He did give His life—for me, for you.

† [Prayer III] "On the night He was betrayed, He... gave You thanks and praise": Not only was Jesus aware that he would endure the physical pain of the Cross, but He also knew that He had to endure the emotional anguish of Judas' betrayal. Still, He gives God thanks and praise. For every type of anguish I have felt—physical, emotional, spiritual—Jesus has traveled the road before me, and can guide my steps to victory.

† [Prayer IV] "When the time came for Him to be glorified by His heavenly Father, He showed the depth of His love": This is the prayer that makes the most sense to my materially oriented mindset. The goal is clear: glory, victory, redemption, love. It is only when I realize that the road to glory intersects a Cross that my thoughts rebel. Jesus it makes clear that the Cross is a necessary stop on the way to salvation.

Which verse touched your heart? Why?

Jesus is truly Present in the Eucharist. What would you like to say to Him when you meet Him again in Communion?

Appendix A:

## Prayers of the Rosary

# The Apostles' Creed

I believe in God, the Father Almighty,
    Creator of heaven and earth.
I believe in Jesus Christ, His only Son, our Lord,
    Who was conceived by the Holy Spirit,
    Born of the Virgin Mary,
    Suffered under Pontius Pilate,
    Was crucified, died, and was buried.
    He descended into hell, rose again on the third day,
    And ascended into heaven.
    He sits at the right hand of God the Father Almighty,
    Thence He shall come to judge the living and the dead.
I believe in the Holy Spirit,
    The holy catholic church,
    The communion of saints,
    The forgiveness of sins,
    The resurrection of the body,
    And the life everlasting.  Amen.

## The Lord's Prayer (Our Father)

Our Father, who art in heaven, hallowed be Thy name.
Thy kingdom come, Thy will be done on earth as it is in heaven.
Give us this day our daily bread,
And forgive us our trespasses as we forgive those who trespass against us.
And lead us not into temptation, but deliver us from evil. Amen.

## Hail Mary

Hail Mary, full of grace, the Lord is with you.
Blessed are you among women, and blessed is the fruit of your womb, Jesus.
Holy Mary, Mother of God,
Pray for us sinners now and at the hour of our death. Amen.

## Glory be to the Father

Glory be to the Father and to the Son and to the Holy Spirit,
As it was in the beginning, is now, and ever shall be, World without end.
Amen.

## Fatima Prayer (O my Jesus, forgive us...)

O my Jesus, forgive us our sins, save us from the fires of hell,
Lead all souls to heaven, especially those in most need of Thy mercy.

## Hail, Holy Queen

Hail, holy Queen, mother of mercy, our life, our sweetness, and our hope. To you do we cry, poor banished children of Eve; to you do we send up our sighs, mourning and weeping in this valley of tears. Turn, then, most gracious advocate, your eyes of mercy toward us, and after this, our exile, show unto us the blessed fruit of your womb, Jesus. O clement, O loving, O sweet virgin Mary: pray for us, O holy Mother of God, that we may be made worthy of the promises of Christ. Amen.

Appendix B:

## A Scriptural Rosary from the Book of Psalms and the Book of Sirach

## The First Joyful Mystery:
### The Annunciation of Gabriel to Mary

*Our Father*

† [Happy the man who] the law of the LORD is their joy;
  God's law they study day and night.
                    *Psalm 1:2*        *(Lk 1:26,27)*     *Hail Mary*

† I will proclaim the decree of the LORD,
  who said to me, "You are my son;
  today I am your father."
                    *Psalm 2:7*        *(Lk 1:30,31)*    *Hail Mary*

† Safety comes from the LORD!
  Your blessing for your people!
                    *Psalm 3:9*        *(Lk 1:32)*       *Hail Mary*

† Know that the LORD works wonders for the faithful;
  the LORD hears when I call out.
                    *Psalm 4:4*        *(Lk 1:34)*       *Hail Mary*

† But I can enter your house
  because of your great love.
  I can worship in your holy temple
  because of my reverence for you, LORD.
                    *Psalm 5:8*        *(Lk 1:35)*       *Hail Mary*

† The LORD has heard my prayer;
  the LORD takes up my plea.
                    *Psalm 6:10*       *(Lk 1:36)*       *Hail Mary*

† O LORD, judge of the nations.
  Grant me justice, LORD, for I am blameless,
  free of any guilt.
                    *Psalm 7:9*        *(Lk 1:26-28)*    *Hail Mary*

† O LORD, our Lord,
  how awesome is your name through all the earth!
  You have set your majesty above the heavens!
                    *Psalm 8:2*        *(Lk 1:32)*       *Hail Mary*

† Those who honor your name trust in you;
  a stronghold in times of trouble.
                    *Psalm 9:11*       *(Lk 1:37)*       *Hail Mary*

† The LORD is king forever;
  the nations have vanished from God's land.
                    *Psalm 10:16*      *(Lk 1:38)*       *Hail Mary*

*Glory be to the Father, ...*
*O my Jesus, forgive us...*

## The Second Joyful Mystery:
## **The Visitation of Mary to Elizabeth**

*Our Father*

† The LORD is in his holy temple;
the LORD's throne is in heaven.
God's eyes keep careful watch,
they test all peoples.
    *Psalm 11:4*        *(Lk 1:41,42)*      **Hail Mary**

† The promises of the LORD are sure,
silver refined in a crucible,
silver purified seven times.
    *Psalm 12:7*        *(Lk 1:45)*      **Hail Mary**

† I trust in your faithfulness.
Grant my heart joy in your help,
That I may sing of the LORD,
"How good our God has been to me!"
    *Psalm 13:6b*        *(Lk 1:46,47)*      **Hail Mary**

† Oh, that from Zion might come
the deliverance of Israel,
That Jacob may rejoice and Israel be glad
when the LORD restores his people!
    *Psalm 14:7*        *(Lk 1:49)*      **Hail Mary**

† Whoever walks without blame,
doing what is right, / speaking truth from the heart.
    *Psalm 15:2*        *(Lk 1:50)*      **Hail Mary**

† Therefore my heart is glad, my soul rejoices;
my body also dwells secure.
    *Psalm 16:9*        *(Lk 1:48)*      **Hail Mary**

† Keep me as the apple of your eye;
hide me in the shadow of your wings.
    *Psalm 17:8*        *(Lk 1:48)*      **Hail Mary**

† Thus I will proclaim you, LORD, among the nations;
I will sing the praises of your name.
    *Psalm 18:50*        *(Lk 1:49)*      **Hail Mary**

† Let the words of my mouth meet with your favor,
keep the thoughts of my heart before you,
LORD, my rock and my redeemer.
    *Psalm 19:15*        *(Lk 1:41,42)*      **Hail Mary**

† Now I know victory is given
to the anointed of the LORD.
God will answer him from the holy heavens
with a strong arm that brings victory.
    *Psalm 20:7*        *(Lk 1:54,55)*      **Hail Mary**

*Glory be to the Father, ...*
*O my Jesus, forgive us...*

## The Third Joyful Mystery:
### The Birth of Jesus

Our Father

† You make him the pattern of blessings forever;
    you gladden him with the joy of your presence.
Psalm 21:7    (Lk 2:6,7)    Hail Mary

† You who fear the LORD, give praise!
    All descendants of Jacob, give honor;
    show reverence, all descendants of Israel!
Psalm 22:24    (Lk 2:8)    Hail Mary

† Only goodness and love will pursue me
    all the days of my life;
    I will dwell in the house of the LORD
      for years to come.
Psalm 23:6    (Lk 2:11)    Hail Mary

† Who is this king of glory?
    The LORD of hosts is the king of glory.
Psalm 24:10    (Lk 2:13,14)    Hail Mary

† Guide me in your truth and teach me,
    for you are God my savior.
    For you I wait all the long day,
      because of your goodness, LORD.
Psalm 25:5    (Mt 2:1,2)    Hail Mary

† Your love is before my eyes;
    I walk guided by your faithfulness.
Psalm 26:3    (Mt 2:10,11)    Hail Mary

† "Come," says my heart, "seek God's face";
    your face, LORD, do I seek!
Psalm 27:8    (Lk 2:15)    Hail Mary

† The LORD is my strength and my shield,
    in whom my heart trusted and found help.
    So my heart rejoices;
      with my song I praise my God.
Psalm 28:7    (Lk 2:20)    Hail Mary

† Give to the LORD the glory due God's name.
    Bow down before the LORD's holy splendor!
Psalm 29:2    (Lk 2:13)    Hail Mary

† With my whole being I sing
    endless praise to you.
    O LORD, my God,
      forever will I give you thanks.
Psalm 30:13    (Lk 2:14)    Hail Mary

Glory be to the Father, ...
O my Jesus, forgive us...

## The Fourth Joyful Mystery:
## **The Presentation in the Temple**

*Our Father*

† Into your hands I commend my spirit;
  you will redeem me, LORD, faithful God.
  Psalm 31:6     (Lk 2:29)     *Hail Mary*

† Be glad in the LORD and rejoice, you just;
  exult, all you upright of heart.
  Psalm 32:11     (Lk 2:25)     *Hail Mary*

† The one who fashioned the hearts of them all
  knows all their works.
  Psalm 33:15     (Lk 2:26)     *Hail Mary*

† Look to God that you may be radiant with joy
  and your faces may not blush for shame.
  Psalm 34:6     (Lk 2:30)     *Hail Mary*

† But let those who favor my just cause
  shout for joy and be glad.
  May they ever say, "Exalted be the LORD
  who delights in the peace of his loyal servant."
  Psalm 35:27     (Lk 2:28)     *Hail Mary*

† Continue your kindness toward your friends,
  your just defense of the honest heart.
  Psalm 36:11     (Lk 2:38)     *Hail Mary*

† The salvation of the just is from the LORD,
  their refuge in time of distress.
  Psalm 37:39     (Lk 2:32)     *Hail Mary*

† LORD, I wait for you;
  O Lord, my God, answer me.
  Psalm 38:16     (Lk 2:25)     *Hail Mary*

† And now, Lord, what future do I have?
  You are my only hope.
  Psalm 39:8     (Lk 2:26)     *Hail Mary*

† I waited, waited for the LORD,
  who bent down and heard my cry.
  Psalm 40:2     (Lk 2:29)     *Hail Mary*

*Glory be to the Father, ...*
*O my Jesus, forgive us...*

## The Fifth Joyful Mystery:
### The Finding of Jesus in the Temple

*Our Father*

† For my integrity you have supported me
   and let me stand in your presence forever.
   Psalm 41:13    (Lk 2:40)    *Hail Mary*

† Those times I recall
      as I pour out my soul,
   When I went in procession with the crowd,
      I went with them to the house of God,
   Amid loud cries of thanksgiving,
      with the multitude keeping festival.
   Psalm 42:5    (Lk 2:41,42)    *Hail Mary*

† That I may come to the altar of God,
      to God, my joy, my delight.
   Then I will praise you with the harp,
      O God, my God.
   Psalm 43:4    (Lk 2:43)    *Hail Mary*

† O God, we have heard with our own ears;
      our ancestors have told us
   The deeds you did in their days,
      with your own hand in days of old.
   Psalm 44:2    (Lk 2:46)    *Hail Mary*

† I will make your name renowned through all generations;
      the nations shall praise you forever.
   Psalm 45:18    (Lk 2:47)    *Hail Mary*

† Come and see the works of the LORD,
      who has done fearsome deeds on earth.
   Psalm 46:9    (Lk 2:50)    *Hail Mary*

† Who chose a land for our heritage,
      the glory of Jacob, the beloved.
   Psalm 47:5    (Lk 2:49)    *Hail Mary*

† O God, within your temple
      we ponder your steadfast love.
   Psalm 48:10    (Lk 2:47)    *Hail Mary*

† My mouth shall speak wisdom,
      my heart shall offer insight.
   Psalm 49:4    (Lk 2:52)    *Hail Mary*

† "Listen, my people, I will speak;
      Israel, I will testify against you;
   God, your God, am I."
   Psalm 50:7    (Lk 2:46,47)    *Hail Mary*

*Glory be to the Father, ...*
*O my Jesus, forgive us...*

# The First Sorrowful Mystery:
## The Agony in the Garden

*Our Father*

† Do not drive me from your presence,
    nor take from me your holy spirit.
        Psalm 51:13    (Lk 22:40)    *Hail Mary*

† But I, like an olive tree in the house of God,
    trust in God's faithful love forever.
        Psalm 52:10    (Mt 26:39)    *Hail Mary*

† Oh, that from Zion might come
    the deliverance of Israel,
  That Jacob may rejoice and Israel be glad
    when God restores the people!
        Psalm 53:7    (Jn 18:4-5)    *Hail Mary*

† God is present as my helper; / the Lord sustains my life.
        Psalm 54:6    (Lk 22:43)    *Hail Mary*

† If an enemy had reviled me,
    that I could bear;
  If my foe had viewed me with contempt,
    from that I could hide.
  [But not from] you, whose company I enjoyed;
    at whose side I walked
    in procession in the house of God!
        Psalm 55:13,15(Lk 22:47,48)    *Hail Mary*

† They hide together in ambush;
    they watch my every step;
    they lie in wait for my life.
        Psalm 56:7    (Lk 22:1-2)    *Hail Mary*

† They have set a trap for my feet;
    my soul is bowed down;
  They have dug a pit before me.
    May they fall into it themselves!
        Psalm 57:7    (Lk 22:3-4)    *Hail Mary*

† Do you indeed pronounce justice, O gods;
    do you judge mortals fairly?
  No, you freely engage in crime;
    your hands dispense violence to the earth.
        Psalm 58:2,3    (Mk 14:63,64)    *Hail Mary*

† They have set an ambush for my life;
    the powerful conspire against me.
  For no offense or misdeed of mine, LORD.
        Psalm 59:4    (Lk 23:47)    *Hail Mary*

† Give us aid against the foe; / worthless is human help.
        Psalm 60:13    (Mk 14:50)    *Hail Mary*

*Glory be to the Father, ...*
*O my Jesus, forgive us...*

87

## The Second Sorrowful Mystery:
### The Scourging at the Pillar

*Our Father*

† Hear my cry, O God,
  listen to my prayer!
  *Psalm 61:2*          *(Mt 26:64)*          *Hail Mary*

† How long will you set upon people,
  all of you beating them down,
  As though they were a sagging fence
  or a battered wall?
  *Psalm 62:4*          *(Mk 15:15)*          *Hail Mary*

† My soul clings fast to you;
  your right hand upholds me.
  *Psalm 63:9*          *(Jn 18:11)*          *Hail Mary*

† They devise wicked schemes,
  conceal the schemes they devise;
  the designs of their hearts are hidden.
  *Psalm 64:7*          *(Mt 27:17,18)*          *Hail Mary*

† We are overcome by our sins;
  only you can pardon them.
  *Psalm 65:4b*          *(Mt 27:25)*          *Hail Mary*

† You led us into a snare;
  you bound us at the waist as captives.
  *Psalm 66:11*          *(Mt 27:20)*          *Hail Mary*

† So shall your rule be known upon the earth,
  your saving power among all the nations.
  *Psalm 67:3*          *(Jn 18:20,21)*          *Hail Mary*

† Blessed be the Lord day by day,
  God, our salvation, who carries us.
  *Psalm 68:20*          *(Mt 8:16,17)*          *Hail Mary*

† Because zeal for your house consumes me,
  I am scorned by those who scorn you.
  *Psalm 69:10*          *(Mk 14:64,65)*          *Hail Mary*

† Graciously rescue me, God!
  Come quickly to help me, LORD!
  *Psalm 70:2*          *(Jn 19:11)*          *Hail Mary*

*Glory be to the Father, ...*
*O my Jesus, forgive us...*

## The Third Sorrowful Mystery:
## The Crowning with Thorns

*Our Father*

† My God, rescue me from the power of the wicked,
    from the clutches of the violent.
                Psalm 71:4      (Mt 27:27)    *Hail Mary*

† May his foes kneel before him,
    his enemies lick the dust.
                Psalm 72:9      (Mk 15:18,19)    *Hail Mary*

† For I am afflicted day after day,
    chastised every morning.
                Psalm 73:14      (Mt 27:28)    *Hail Mary*

† Yet you, God, are my king from of old,
    winning victories throughout the earth.
                Psalm 74:12      (Jn 18:36,37)    *Hail Mary*

† But from God who decides,
    who brings some low and raises others high.
                Psalm 75:8      (Mt 27:24)    *Hail Mary*

† From the heavens you pronounced sentence;
    the earth was terrified and reduced to silence.
                Psalm 76:9      (Mt 17:5,6)    *Hail Mary*

† When I think of God, I groan;
    as I ponder, my spirit grows faint.
                Psalm 77:4      (Jn 19:7,8)    *Hail Mary*

† He gave up his might into captivity,
    his glorious ark into the hands of the foe.
                Psalm 78:61      (Mt 27:29)    *Hail Mary*

† We have become the reproach of our neighbors,
    the scorn and derision of those around us.
                Psalm 79:4      (Mt 27:30)    *Hail Mary*

† You have left us to be fought over by our neighbors;
    our enemies deride us.
O LORD of hosts, restore us;
    let your face shine upon us,
    that we may be saved.
                Psalm 80:7-8      (Mt 27:31)    *Hail Mary*

*Glory be to the Father, ...*
*O my Jesus, forgive us...*

## The Fourth Sorrowful Mystery:
### The Carrying of the Cross

*Our Father*

† In distress you called and I rescued you.
        *Psalm 81:8a*    *(Lk 23:42,43)*    *Hail Mary*

† The gods neither know nor understand,
    wandering about in darkness,
    and all the world's foundations shake.
        *Psalm 82:5*    *(Mt 27:45)*    *Hail Mary*

† See how your enemies rage;
    your foes proudly raise their heads.
        *Psalm 83:3*    *(Mt 27:41)*    *Hail Mary*

† My soul yearns and pines
    for the courts of the LORD.
My heart and flesh cry out
    for the living God.
        *Psalm 84:3*    *(Mt 27:46)*    *Hail Mary*

† You forgave the guilt of your people,
    pardoned all their sins.
        *Psalm 85:3*    *(Lk 23:34)*    *Hail Mary*

† O God, the arrogant have risen against me;
    a ruthless band has sought my life;
    to you they pay no heed.
        *Psalm 86:14*    *(Mt 27:44)*    *Hail Mary*

† The LORD notes in the register of the peoples:
    "This one was born here."
        *Psalm 87:6*    *(Mt 27:54)*    *Hail Mary*

† For my soul is filled with troubles;
    my life draws near to Sheol.
        *Psalm 88:4*    *(Mt 27:50)*    *Hail Mary*

† What mortal can live and not see death?
    Who can escape the power of Sheol?
        *Psalm 89:49*    *(Jn 10:17,18)*    *Hail Mary*

† Make us glad as many days as you humbled us,
    for as many years as we have seen trouble.
        *Psalm 90:15*    *(Rom 5:3-5)*    *Hail Mary*

*Glory be to the Father, ...*
*O my Jesus, forgive us...*

## The Fifth Sorrowful Mystery:
### The Crucifixion

*Our Father*

† Whoever clings to me, I will deliver;
  whoever knows my name I will set on high.
  Psalm 91:14    (Lk 23:43)    *Hail Mary*

† How great are your works, LORD!
  How profound your purpose!
  Psalm 92:6    (Mt 27:50-52)    *Hail Mary*

† Your throne stands firm from of old;
  you are from everlasting, LORD.
  Psalm 93:2    (Jn 8:58)    *Hail Mary*

† If the LORD were not my help,
  I would long have been silent in the grave.
  Psalm 94:17    (Lk 23:46)    *Hail Mary*

† Come, let us sing joyfully to the LORD;
  cry out to the rock of our salvation.
  Psalm 95:1    (Rom 5:11)    *Hail Mary*

† Sing to the LORD, bless his name;
  announce his salvation day after day.
  Psalm 96:2    (Acts 2:38)    *Hail Mary*

† The LORD loves those who hate evil,
  protects the lives of the faithful,
  rescues them from the hand of the wicked.
  Psalm 97:10    (Jn 19:26,27)    *Hail Mary*

† The LORD has made his victory known;
  has revealed his triumph for the nations to see.
  Psalm 98:2    (Acts 2:23,24)    *Hail Mary*

† O LORD, our God, you answered them;
  you were a forgiving God,
  though you punished their offenses.
  Psalm 99:8    (Jn 3:17)    *Hail Mary*

† Good indeed is the LORD,
  Whose love endures forever,
  whose faithfulness lasts through every age.
  Psalm 100:5    (Rev 7:11,12)    *Hail Mary*

*Glory be to the Father, ...*
*O my Jesus, forgive us...*

## The First Glorious Mystery:
### The Resurrection of the Lord

*Our Father*

† I look to the faithful of the land;
 they alone can be my companions.
 Those who follow the way of integrity,
 they alone can enter my service.
 *Psalm 101:6* *(Mt 28:9)* *Hail Mary*

† You will again show mercy to Zion;
 now is the time for pity;
 the appointed time has come.
 *Psalm 102:14* *(Lk 24:1,3)* *Hail Mary*

† [He] delivers your life from the pit,
 surrounds you with love and compassion.
 *Psalm 103:4* *(Lk 24:46,47)* *Hail Mary*

† When you send forth your breath, they are created,
 and you renew the face of the earth.
 *Psalm 104:30* *(Lk 24:32)* *Hail Mary*

† His prediction came to pass,
 and the word of the LORD proved him true.
 *Psalm 105:19* *(Lk 24:44,45)* *Hail Mary*

† That I may see the prosperity of your chosen,
 rejoice in the joy of your people,
 and glory with your heritage.
 *Psalm 106:5* *(Mk 16:17,18)* *Hail Mary*

† [He] sent forth the word to heal them,
 snatched them from the grave.
 Let them thank the LORD for such kindness,
 such wondrous deeds for mere mortals.
 *Psalm 107:20,21* *(Mt 28:19)* *Hail Mary*

† Awake, my soul; awake, lyre and harp!
 I will wake the dawn.
 *Psalm 108:3* *(Mt 28:1)* *Hail Mary*

† Make them know this is your hand,
 that you, LORD, have acted.
 *Psalm 109:27* *(Mk 16:6)* *Hail Mary*

† The scepter of your sovereign might
 the LORD will extend from Zion.
 The LORD says: "Rule over your enemies!"
 *Psalm 110:2* *(Mt 28:18)* *Hail Mary*

*Glory be to the Father, ...*
*O my Jesus, forgive us...*

## The Second Glorious Mystery:
### The Ascension of Jesus into Heaven

*Our Father*

† You showed powerful deeds to your people,
giving them the lands of the nations.
Psalm 111:6    (Jn 20:30,31)    *Hail Mary*

† They shine through the darkness, a light for the upright;
they are gracious, merciful, and just.
Psalm 112:4    (Jn 12:35,36)    *Hail Mary*

† Who is like the LORD,
our God enthroned on high,
looking down on heaven and earth?
Psalm 113:5,6    (Mk 16:19)    *Hail Mary*

† Tremble, earth, before the Lord,
before the God of Jacob.
Psalm 114:7    (Rev 1:12-17)    *Hail Mary*

† Not to us, LORD, not to us
but to your name give glory
because of your faithfulness and love.
Psalm 115:1    (Phil 2:9)    *Hail Mary*

† I shall walk before the LORD
in the land of the living.
Psalm 116:9    (Jn 11:25-27)    *Hail Mary*

† Praise the LORD, all you nations!
Give glory, all you peoples!
The LORD's love for us is strong;
the LORD is faithful forever.
Hallelujah!
Psalm 117:1,2    (Acts 2:38,39)    *Hail Mary*

† Open the gates of victory;
I will enter and thank the LORD.
Psalm 118:19    (Heb 12:2)    *Hail Mary*

† Your word, LORD, stands forever;
it is firm as the heavens.
Psalm 119:89    (Jn 1:1,2)    *Hail Mary*

† Too long did I live
among those who hated peace.
Psalm 120:6    (Jn 20:19)    *Hail Mary*

*Glory be to the Father, ...*
*O my Jesus, forgive us...*

## The Third Glorious Mystery:
### The Descent of the Holy Spirit

*Our Father*

† The LORD is your guardian;
   the LORD is your shade
   at your right hand.
                    *Psalm 121:5*     *(Acts 2:36)*     *Hail Mary*

† [To Jerusalem] the tribes have come,
   the tribes of the LORD,
   As it was decreed for Israel,
      to give thanks to the name of the LORD.
                    *Psalm 122:4*     *(Acts 2:1,5)*     *Hail Mary*

† To you I raise my eyes,
   to you enthroned in heaven.
                    *Psalm 123:1*     *(Mk 16:19)*     *Hail Mary*

† Our help is in the name of the LORD,
   the maker of heaven and earth.
                    *Psalm 124:8*     *(Acts 17:24,25)*     *Hail Mary*

† As mountains surround Jerusalem,
   the LORD surrounds his people
   both now and forever.
                    *Psalm 125:2*     *(Acts 2:17)*     *Hail Mary*

† Our mouths were filled with laughter;
   our tongues sang for joy.
   Then it was said among the nations,
      "The LORD has done great things for them."
                    *Psalm 126:2*     *(Acts 2:4)*     *Hail Mary*

† Unless the LORD build the house,
   they labor in vain who build.
   Unless the LORD guard the city,
      in vain does the guard keep watch.
                    *Psalm 127:1*     *(Acts 2:2)*     *Hail Mary*

† Just so will they be blessed
   who fear the LORD.
                    *Psalm 128:4*     *(Acts 1:8)*     *Hail Mary*

† Much have they oppressed me from my youth,
   yet they have not prevailed.
                    *Psalm 129:2*     *(Rom 8:18)*     *Hail Mary*

† Let Israel look for the LORD,
   For with the LORD is kindness,
   with him is full redemption.
                    *Psalm 130:7*     *(Rom 9:6,15)*     *Hail Mary*

*Glory be to the Father, ...*
*O my Jesus, forgive us...*

## The Fourth Glorious Mystery:
### The Assumption of Mary into Heaven

*Our Father*

† LORD, my heart is not proud;
  nor are my eyes haughty.
I do not busy myself with great matters,
  with things too sublime for me.
  Psalm 131:1     (Rom 12:2)     *Hail Mary*

† "This is my resting place forever;
  here will I dwell, for I desire it."
  Psalm 132:14     (Jn 10:28)     *Hail Mary*

† How good it is, how pleasant,
  where the people dwell as one!
  Psalm 133:1     (Rom 1:11,12)     *Hail Mary*

† Come, bless the LORD,
  all you servants of the LORD
Who stand in the house of the LORD
  through the long hours of night.
  Psalm 134:1     (Jn 12:26)     *Hail Mary*

† Whatever the LORD wishes,
  he does in heaven and on earth,
  in the seas and in all the deeps.
  Psalm 135:6     (Phil 3:20,21)     *Hail Mary*

† Praise the God of heaven,
  God's love endures forever.
  Psalm 136:26     (Eph 2:4-7)     *Hail Mary*

† But how could we sing a song of the LORD
  in a foreign land?
  Psalm 137:4     (Eph 2:19)     *Hail Mary*

† The LORD is with me to the end.
  LORD, your love endures forever.
  Never forsake the work of your hands!
  Psalm 138:8     (Acts 2:27)     *Hail Mary*

† I praise you, so wonderfully you made me;
  wonderful are your works!
My very self you knew.
  Psalm 139:14     (1 Cor 15:22,23)     *Hail Mary*

† Then the just will give thanks to your name;
  the upright will dwell in your presence.
  Psalm 140:14     (Acts 2:28)     *Hail Mary*

*Glory be to the Father, ...*
*O my Jesus, forgive us...*

## The Fifth Glorious Mystery:
### The Coronation of Mary as Queen of Heaven

*Our Father*

† Let my prayer be incense before you;
   my uplifted hands an evening sacrifice.
   Psalm 141:2    (Rom 12:1)    *Hail Mary*

† Lead me out of my prison,
   that I may give thanks to your name.
   Then the just shall gather around me
   because you have been good to me.
   Psalm 142:8    (Heb 12:1)    *Hail Mary*

† Teach me to do your will,
   for you are my God.
   May your kind spirit guide me
   on ground that is level.
   Psalm 143:10    (Jn 14:26)    *Hail Mary*

† Happy the people so blessed;
   happy the people whose God is the LORD.
   Psalm 144:15    (Jn 14:1-3)    *Hail Mary*

† Your reign is a reign for all ages,
   your dominion for all generations.
   Psalm 145:13    (Rev 7:11,12)    *Hail Mary*

† Praise the LORD, my soul;
   I shall praise the LORD all my life,
   sing praise to my God while I live.
   Psalm 146:2    (1 Thess. 5:9,10)    *Hail Mary*

† Rather the LORD takes pleasure in the devout,
   those who await his faithful care.
   Psalm 147:11    (Jam 1:12)    *Hail Mary*

† Let them all praise the LORD's name,
   for his name alone is exalted,
   majestic above earth and heaven.
   Psalm 148:13    (Rom 11:36)    *Hail Mary*

† For the LORD takes delight in his people,
   honors the poor with victory.
   Psalm 149:4    (2 Tim 4:7)    *Hail Mary*

† Give praise for his mighty deeds,
   praise him for his great majesty.
   Psalm 150:2    (Rev 5:13)    *Hail Mary*

*Glory be to the Father, ...*
*O my Jesus, forgive us...*
*Hail, Holy Queen, ...*

## The First Luminous Mystery:
### The Baptism of the Lord

*Our Father*

† Before all things else wisdom was created;
    and prudent understanding, from eternity.
        *Sirach 1:4*     *(Jn 1:1,14)*    *Hail Mary*

† Trust God and he will help you;
    make straight your ways and hope in him.
        *Sirach 2:6*     *(Lk 3:3,4)*    *Hail Mary*

† Humble yourself the more, the greater you are,
    and you will find favor with God.
        *Sirach 3:18*     *(Mt 3:13)*    *Hail Mary*

† Refrain not from speaking at the proper time,
    and hide not away your wisdom.
        *Sirach 4:23*     *(Jn 1:29)*    *Hail Mary*

† Delay not your conversion to the LORD,
    put it not off from day to day.
        *Sirach 5:8*     *(Mt 3:2,8)*    *Hail Mary*

† For he who fears God behaves accordingly,
    and his friend will be like himself.
        *Sirach 6:17*     *(Mk 1:7,8)*    *Hail Mary*

† With all your strength, love your Creator,
    forsake not his ministers.
        *Sirach 7:30*     *(Mt 3:14,15)*    *Hail Mary*

† Spurn not the discourse of the wise,
    but acquaint yourself with their proverbs;
    From them you will acquire the training
    to serve in the presence of princes.
        *Sirach 8:8*     *(Lk 3:10)*    *Hail Mary*

† With the learned be intimate;
    let all your conversation be about the law of the LORD.
        *Sirach 9:15*     *(Mk 1:8,9)*    *Hail Mary*

† My son, with humility have self-esteem;
    prize yourself as you deserve.
        *Sirach 10:27*     *(Mt 3:16,17)*    *Hail Mary*

*Glory be to the Father, ...*
*O my Jesus, forgive us...*

## The Second Luminous Mystery:
### The Miracle of Cana

*Our Father*

† God's blessing is the lot of the just man,
and in due time his hopes bear fruit.
*Sirach 11:22*     *(Jn 2:1a,2)*     *Hail Mary*

† If you do good, know for whom you are doing it,
and your kindness will have its effect.
*Sirach 12:1*     *(Jn 2:3)*     *Hail Mary*

† Be not bold with [a man of influence] lest you be rebuffed,
but keep not too far away lest you be forgotten.
*Sirach 13:10*     *(Jn 2:4)*     *Hail Mary*

† Before you die, be good to your friend,
and give him a share in what you possess.
*Sirach 14:13*     *(Jn 2:5)*     *Hail Mary*

† The eyes of God see all he has made;
he understands man's every deed.
*Sirach 15:19*     *(Jn 2:6,7)*     *Hail Mary*

† Then the LORD looked upon the earth,
and filled it with his blessings.
*Sirach 16:27*     *(Jn 2:8)*     *Hail Mary*

† His majestic glory their eyes beheld,
his glorious voice their ears heard.
*Sirach 17:11*     *(Jn 2:11)*     *Hail Mary*

† Whom has he made equal to describing his works,
and who can probe his mighty deeds?
*Sirach 18:2*     *(Jn 2:9)*     *Hail Mary*

† Tell nothing to friend or foe;
if you have a fault, reveal it not.
*Sirach 19:7*     *(Jn 2:10a)*     *Hail Mary*

† Some misfortunes bring success;
some things gained are a man's loss.
*Sirach 20:8*     *(Jn 2:10b)*     *Hail Mary*

*Glory be to the Father, ...*
*O my Jesus, forgive us...*

The Third Luminous Mystery:
## The Proclamation of the Kingdom of God

*Our Father*

† A wise man's knowledge wells up in a flood,
   and his counsel, like a living spring.
   Sirach 21:13     (Jn 6:14)     *Hail Mary*

† A resolve that is backed by prudent understanding
   is like the polished surface of a smooth wall.
   Sirach 22:17     (Mt 13:23)     *Hail Mary*

† Thus all who dwell on the earth shall know,
   and all who inhabit the world shall understand,
   That nothing is better than the fear of the LORD,
   nothing more salutary than to obey his commandments.
   Sirach 23:27     (Mt 22:37,38)     *Hail Mary*

† He who obeys me will not be put to shame;
   he who serves me will never fail.
   Sirach 24:21     (Mt 5:11,12)     *Hail Mary*

† With three things I am delighted,
   for they are pleasing to the LORD and to men:
   Harmony among brethren, friendship among neighbors,
   and the mutual love of husband and wife.
   Sirach 25:1     (Mt 19:6)     *Hail Mary*

† [The man who fears the Lord,] be he rich or poor, his heart is content,
   and a smile is ever on his face.
   Sirach 26:4     (Mt 11:28-30)     *Hail Mary*

† The fruit of a tree shows the care it has had;
   so too does a man's speech disclose the bent of his mind.
   Sirach 27:6     (Mt 7:16,17)     *Hail Mary*

† Think of the commandments, hate not your neighbor;
   of the Most High's covenant, and overlook faults.
   Sirach 28:7     (Mt 7:12)     *Hail Mary*

† Dispose of your treasure as the Most High commands,
   for that will profit you more than the gold.
   Sirach 29:11     (Lk 12:33)     *Hail Mary*

† At [his] death, he will seem not dead,
   since he leaves after him one like himself.
   Sirach 30:4     (Jn 16:13)     *Hail Mary*

*Glory be to the Father, ...*
*O my Jesus, forgive us ...*

# The Fourth Luminous Mystery:
## The Transfiguration

*Our Father*

† Who is he, that we may praise him?
He, of all his kindred, has done wonders, ...
    and this remains his glory;
He could have sinned but did not,
    could have done evil but would not.
        *Sirach 31:9a,10*   *(Lk 9:29)*   *Hail Mary*

† Above all, give praise to your Creator,
    who showers his favors upon you.
        *Sirach 32:13*   *(Lk 9:32)*   *Hail Mary*

† Like clay in the hands of a potter,
    to be molded according to his pleasure,
So are men in the hands of their Creator,
    to be assigned by him their function.
        *Sirach 33:13*   *(Lk 9:34,35)*   *Hail Mary*

† Lively is the courage of those who fear the LORD,
    for they put their hope in their savior.
        *Sirach 34:13*   *(Lk 9:33)*   *Hail Mary*

† He who serves God willingly is heard;
    his petition reaches the heavens.
        *Sirach 35:16*   *(Lk 9:35 )*   *Hail Mary*

† Reward those who have hoped in you,
    and let your prophets be proved true.
Hear the prayer of your servants,
    for you are ever gracious to your people;
Thus it will be known to the very ends of the earth
    that you are the eternal God.
        *Sirach 36:15-17*   *(Mt 17:5)*   *Hail Mary*

† Most important of all, pray to God / to set your feet in the path of truth.
        *Sirach 37:15*   *(Mt 17:7)*   *Hail Mary*

† Thus God's creative work continues without cease
    in its efficacy on the surface of the earth.
        *Sirach 38:8*   *(Lk 9:37)*   *Hail Mary*

† Many will praise his understanding; / his fame can never be effaced;
Unfading will be his memory, / through all generations his name will live.
        *Sirach 39:9*   *(Mt 17:3)*   *Hail Mary*

† But goodness will never be cut off, / and justice endures forever.
Wealth or wages can make life sweet,
    but better than either is finding a treasure.
        *Sirach 40:17*   *(Mt 17:20b)*   *Hail Mary*

*Glory be to the Father, ...*
*O my Jesus, forgive us...*

## The Fifth Luminous Mystery:
## **The Institution of the Holy Eucharist**

*Our Father*

† Man's body is a fleeting thing,
   but a virtuous name will never be annihilated.
                    *Sirach 41:11*      *(Mk 14:9)*        *Hail Mary*

† Now will I recall God's works;
   what I have seen, I will describe.
   At God's word were his works brought into being;
   they do his will as he has ordained for them.
                    *Sirach 42:15*      *(1 Cor. 11:23)*   *Hail Mary*

† It is the LORD who has made all things,
   and to those who fear him he gives wisdom.
                    *Sirach 43:35*      *(Jn 6:57)*        *Hail Mary*

† He observed the precepts of the Most High,
   and entered into an agreement with him.
                    *Sirach 44:20a*     *(Lk 22:13-14)*    *Hail Mary*

† He made him perpetual in his office
   when he bestowed on him the priesthood of his people;
   He established him in honor
   and crowned him with lofty majesty.
                    *Sirach 45:7*       *(1 Cor. 11:25b)*  *Hail Mary*

† Beloved of his people, dear to his Maker,
   dedicated from his mother's womb,
   Consecrated to the LORD.
                    *Sirach 46:13a*     *(Mk 15:39)*       *Hail Mary*

† But God does not withdraw his mercy,
   nor permit even one of his promises to fail.
   He does not uproot the posterity of his chosen one,
   nor destroy the offspring of his friend.
   So he gave to Jacob a remnant,
   to David a root from his own family.
                    *Sirach 47:22*      *(Mk 10:47)*       *Hail Mary*

† Blessed is he who shall have seen you before he dies.
                    *Sirach 48:11*      *(Lk 23:42-43)*    *Hail Mary*

† He turned to God with his whole heart,
   and, though times were evil, he practiced virtue.
                    *Sirach 49:3*       *(Heb 4:15)*       *Hail Mary*

† All the people of the land would shout for joy,
   praying to the Merciful One,
   As the high priest completed the services at the altar
   by presenting to God the sacrifice due.
                    *Sirach 50:19*      *(Lk 23:47)*       *Hail Mary*

*Glory be to the Father, ...*
*O my Jesus, forgive us...*

4870750R0

Made in the USA
Charleston, SC
29 March 2010